MW01603076

Pearls:
Women Who Radiate Success
Book II

By Fred Dawson

with Dana Dobson

Pearls: Women Who Radiate Success © 2017 by Fred Dawson

All rights reserved. No part of this book may be reproduced, stored in a retrieval system or transmitted in any form by any means without the prior written permission of the publishers, except by a reviewer who may quote brief passages in a review to be printed in a newspaper or journal.

ISBN 978-1-48359-946-5

Printed in the United States of America

I believe in strong women. I believe in the woman who is able to stand up for herself. I believe in the woman who doesn't need to hide behind her husband's back. I believe that if you have problems, as a woman you deal with them, you don't play victim, you don't make yourself look pitiful, you don't point fingers. You stand and you deal. You face the world with a head held high and you carry the universe in your heart.

—C. JoyBell C.

Table of Contents

Foreword

Most of us have many associates, colleagues or acquaintances. But we don't have many actual friends — and Facebook doesn't count. How many people can you say you *completely* trust, admire and respect?

Fred Dawson is a real friend and a rare breed. He's fabulously successful yet genuine, kind and distinctively generous. And even though his band, Club Phred, in which Fred plays a mean Hammond B-3 organ, has raised millions for charity, Fred has no ego. By day, he's a respected financial planner, but by night, weekend and any other openings he has left after spending time with his family, he's supporting myriad organizations, including Great Dames, Inc. and the Fresh Start Scholarship Foundation, both of which have helped thousands of women make better lives for themselves. Fred has mentored colleagues of mine, all of whom say he changed their lives. I believe that his deep love and respect for his mother led to his lifelong support of women. He was a loving son who became a great man, and because of the wonderful woman who raised him, he learned to honor women as equals.

Fred and I go way back. For years, I have witnessed him give unceremoniously of his time and resources. Yes, he does love his rock 'n' roll, and he still gushes like a teenager when he hears that downbeat. But I think Fred is happier behind the scenes. He seeks no glory for his generosity. He realizes that those with much must nurture those with little.

I was humbled when Fred invited me to be featured with several other women in the first "Pearls" book, and thrilled to serve as editor for this sequel. The incredible women you're about to meet shared their thoughts, ambitions, dreams and triumphs. The also spoke bravely of their challenges. What inspired me most was the way they combatted injustice with intellect and talent. I guess that's why Fred calls them "pearls."

I am most grateful to have been a part of this book, but far more appreciative of my friendship with Fred Dawson. His support of women is legend. His altruism is unmatched.

To quote Albert Einstein, "The value of a man resides in what he gives and not in what he is capable of receiving." I'm sure that Einstein would consider Fred a true gentleman, as do I.

Please enjoy the book.

Dr. Maria Hess
Director of Publications
Editor-in-Chief, WilmU Magazine Adjunct
Professor, Wilmington University

Acknowledgments

A book like this does not happen by itself overnight. As a continuation of Book 1, Book II tells more impressive stories by some equally impressive women! I very much appreciate their willingness to open up and share their stories

Thank you, very much, to these "pearls." Dana and I hope that other women will read your stories and get inspired to go on to even greater things.

Deepest thanks to my writer, Dana Dobson, my editor, Dr. Maria Hess, my photographer, Bob Horton from Creative Image Associates, Ara Atkinson-Skinner from Ara Illustrated Studio Group for her book cover and internal design, and Mary Konwinski, who proofread all of this, because spelling counts!

My wife, Louise, has been a woman "in front" of her man, putting up with my rants, raves and rock and roll (did I mention I play in a rock and roll band, too?). I would be remiss if I didn't acknowledge the unconditional love of the delightful, four-legged lady in our home, Daphne—a spring-loaded wire-haired fox terrier.

Marguerite June Dawson

Introduction

This book is part two of a series telling the stories of several women who have displayed great courage, character and determination. I'm fascinated by how these remarkable, high-achieving women, while plodding through life's trials, tragedies, triumphs and terrors (as we all do) continue to carry on, brilliantly, and never lose their faith in humanity.

The series is dedicated to June Dawson, my mother, a single divorcee who worked for years on an automobile assembly line, enduring the taunts and jibes of her male co-workers with unflappable dignity and grace so that her three boys could grow up feeling safe and loved.

I've been asked what criteria I use in selecting the women who are the "Pearls" referred to in the book's title.

First, I asked around. As someone who has lived most of his life in the Philadelphia area, I am lucky to have made hundreds of friends. There's a phenomenon in Delaware we laughingly call, "the two degrees of separation." The joke originates from the play and movie called, "Six Degrees of Separation," which suggests that by virtue of people's connection to one another, we can contact virtually anyone on the planet with a minimum of six steps—a sort of "whisper down the lane."

Delaware is small, so to connect with someone important only takes two steps. Finding these women's names, then, was the easy part. Of course, I've known many of these women for years. The next step was to reach out and ask for an interview. That was the hard part.

As busy as these women are, though, they accepted my invitation with the same goal in mind—to help and reassure other women so that they, too, can find meaning, reassurance and purpose in their own lives. In other words, their willingness to bare their souls is a loving act of service.

Thank you all for the privilege of sharing your stories.

—Fred Dawson

Patricia Beebe

Patricia Beebe

"I am a stronger leader because I have been true to my gender."

Biography

Patricia Dobbe Beebe is the President & CEO of the Food Bank of Delaware. In this role, she oversees a multi-million dollar annual budget and leads a staff of more than 50 employees to ensure the success of the Food Bank's hunger relief, workforce development and public policy programs. The Food Bank of Delaware's network of 625 Hunger-Relief Partners receives more than 900,000 visits annually.

During her tenure, Patricia envisioned and implemented two 14-week professional culinary training certificate programs, operating out of both the nonprofit's Newark and Milford locations. These culinary schools move beyond traditional hunger relief efforts to provide workforce development training opportunities to more than 90 unemployed and under-employed individuals and community members re-entering society from correctional facilities each year.

With more than 30 years of experience in the human services field, Patricia has an extensive background in new program development, strategic planning, fund management, grant writing, public policy and personnel management. Prior to assuming her current role in 1997, Patricia served as the regional director of the Lutheran Services of the South, Inc. She managed 30 multi-disciplinary professional staff at eight office locations in West Texas. She holds a bachelor of science degree and two master's degrees from the University of Wisconsin-Madison.

Patricia resides in Chadds Ford, Pa., with her husband, Donald, and has two adult children. She's a committed animal rights person, with two dogs and five cats, most of them rescued. In her spare time, she enjoys reading, spending time outdoors and traveling.

Patricia's Story

Patricia Beebe says she was born outside the box, much to the good fortune of anyone who cannot afford to feed their family or suffers from harsh life circumstances. She believes strongly in second chances. She's been given a few herself, and through the years she has come to see food as a catalyst for change and redemption.

In the early 2000s, she asked her team at The Food Bank of Delaware a pivotal question: What *more* could we be doing for people that goes beyond just providing emergency food? How can we re-engineer the concept of food assistance beyond the expected, and thus have a greater positive impact on the community?

And because she was born outside the box, Patricia decided to start a culinary school. Frankly, most of us would never had made such a non-intuitive connection, but to Patricia, the idea made perfect sense. Naturally, policy people and community decision makers scoffed, but true to character, Patricia persevered, and within two years and with limited resources, she opened the culinary school. When the naysayers dropped into the classroom and saw the program's strong focus on culinary arts and listened to the success stories of its students, they sang a different tune.

The culinary school is a place for cooking up second chances. Its students learn how to prepare delicious food and secure jobs in the culinary field. The industry, says Patricia, is very forgiving of people with a past, as long as they're great cooks. She and her team are doing what the rest of the "Pearls" feel led to do: making a difference.

Patricia was born in Stevens Point, Wis., to parents of German and Scandinavian descent. Her sister, Christine, with whom she is very close, was born three-and-a-half years later.

"We lived in a very isolated part of Wisconsin," says Patricia. "It was more than rural—it was the sticks. There were trees and lakes everywhere, so it was a beautiful environment, but it wasn't where I wanted to be for the rest of my life."

Her mother, Edith, graduated from high school but never went to college—as was typical in the 1950s—and never worked outside of the home.

"Our community had very little enthusiasm for women going to college," says Patricia. "My mother devoted herself to taking care of her family and stretching resources as far as possible. She was very smart and extremely creative—was one of those people who could make something out of nothing. She made all of our clothes because we were poor, and she was a talented cook who canned almost everything."

Patricia idolized her father, Roy, an eighth-grade graduate who labored in saw mills, plowed snow, hunted and fished, and took any other odd jobs he could get. Their beef, says Patricia, was deer meat.

"To my sister and me, my dad was the be-all-and-end-all," says Patricia. "He never did anything bad, ever. He was just one of the most genuinely nice people you'd ever want to meet. He was steady and kind, even through all of the hardships."

One of those hardships came when Patricia's mother was diagnosed with rheumatoid arthritis that became so painful and debilitating that she required a wheelchair.

"Her pain affected her view of life and how she parented," says Patricia. "But always, like my father, she was a good person and we were a loving family. There was never any substance abuse or crime in our household. I sometimes think if all parents were like mine, the world would be a better place."

Even as a young child, Patricia knew that she wanted a life different than a life in Mercer, Wisconsin, where she'd lived the first 17 years of her life. She knew that in order to get that life, she'd need to attend college.

"If I stayed there, I knew I'd just get married to a local and that would be it," she says. "Maybe that was all right for some people, but not for me. I was always that person who was looking for more, and it didn't make me very popular. Even now in my work I don't really do all the things one is supposed to do—those things considered proper and nice. I'm not afraid to push."

Patricia knew that becoming the person she wanted to be involved taking the chance to figure out a way to afford to go to college. At the time, schools in northern Wisconsin didn't offer much in the way of career counseling, so Patricia took her cues from a mentor, Elvina Finn, who was one of her teachers.

"The belief in the early 1960s was that if you were a woman, you had two career choices," Patricia explains, "teacher, or nurse. Elvina was a teacher, so she helped me enroll in college. In fact, she drove me to the University of Wisconsin herself. And as it turned out, my major was home economics with a minor in art. Those were Elvina's majors, so they became mine. One was practical, and the other— well, wasn't. If I had it to do over again, I would have majored in art, because that was really *me*."

She wound up getting her master's in art, so it all worked out. Later, she earned a second master's in rehabilitation psychology, a program of coursework that she was able to design herself with the help of a professor.

While still an undergraduate, between her junior and senior years, Patricia married Donald Beebe, her husband of 48 years.

"He knew he was going to be drafted because the draft board back then was pretty brutal," says Patricia. "We thought we could either move to Canada, which we didn't feel was the right thing to do, or that he should enlist, which he did. He went to Officer Candidate School and was commissioned a second lieutenant. He was sent to Vietnam and when he came back, he faced public animosity."

Patricia and Don went to graduate school together at the University of Wisconsin at Madison.

"Don was active with the veterans against the Vietnam War," she says. "I became an activist, too, and also a strong feminist. Oh, my! You'll never meet anybody who is as strong-willed and as opinionated as I am. My husband stayed with me, though, and used to say, jokingly, 'I liked you better before you became a feminist.'"

Patricia says she is still an activist, only these days, she doesn't get tear-gassed, nor does she have a bumper sticker that says, "The population bomb is everyone's baby." As a feminist who continues to champion equal opportunities for women, Patricia is well-versed on the topic of gender discrimination.

"First of all, women make $.78 for every dollar a man makes," she says. "Women are still perceived as not having a head for business. I know there were a couple of jobs that I wasn't hired for because I am a woman. If I'm criticized for anything, it's that I'm too aggressive, that I'm not soft enough. I cannot tell you how many times I've been lectured about catching more bees with honey. I wish I had a quarter for every time someone said that to me."

While Don was in Vietnam, Patricia worked for the Virginia Commission for the Visually Impaired in Washington, D.C.

"One of my earlier jobs had been helping people perfect their skills in order remain independent," she says. "I also helped them with their résumés. In the early-to mid-1960s, the popular view was that there was no place for the disabled in the workplace. I never saw disabilities. I saw people who needed to learn new skills so they could get on with their lives. Eighty percent of the people I work with now are from the correctional system."

As an "angel" to the visually impaired, Patricia visited people in their homes and helped them become more self-sufficient. She taught them how to read Braille and how to label their cabinets.

"We also put labels on their clothes so that they'd know how to match outfits," she says. "Whatever they needed, I helped them with. It was an interesting experience. One day I'd be in the Blue Ridge Mountains working with people who were totally impoverished, and the next day I'd be in an upscale neighborhood, greeted at the door by a butler. I'm comfortable talking to anybody. It doesn't matter—I don't get intimidated. I meet people where they are."

Patricia and Don moved often because of his work. Don is a food microbiologist, or food chemist.

"Don makes cereal that doesn't absorb milk, and therefore, doesn't get soggy," says Patricia. She watched my face for my reaction, expecting shock, I think. "Not really," she confirmed. "He's had different jobs in the food industry, doing quality assurance and research at first, and then transitioned to marketing and sales."

They've lived in Texas, Minnesota, Virginia, Massachusetts, Wisconsin and Delaware.

"I was always the traveling spouse," explains Patricia. "So my job was to get the kids acclimated, enroll them in school and find a doctor. After six months, I'd get bored and get a job. I've never wanted to be the woman who doesn't work outside of the home."

When her daughter, Lauren, entered her sophomore year in high school and her son was in grade school, Patricia jumped at the opportunity get back to work.

"I was hot!" she says. "My resume shows that I'm good at raising money and developing new programs. When we were in Texas, I had done a lot of social services fundraising for welfare reform and this

5

was a hot commodity in Delaware in 1997. I had so many job offers I couldn't believe it! I accepted the position at the Food Bank because there were several challenges I wanted to take on."

Patricia is an effective leader, which is evident by the groundbreaking programs she's originated at the Food Bank of Delaware—programs that took a lot of convincing and much teamwork from people who were inspired to support her vision—as "out of the box" as it seemed. It's not only her powers of persuasion that sets her apart: She's also a good manager.

"I am true to my gender, which means that women have a certain way of managing that differs from men," she says. "I don't believe in rules and policies to define how you need to operate. I like to provide a basic structure, and give people the opportunity to do their thing. I'll step in if things get too far off track, and I have a good sense of when there's a problem before anyone tells me about it. I never feel that I have to watch everything that's going on too closely, because in fact, I do know what's going on. I want people to be happy and to give them the power and freedom to make a contribution, to feel that they're accomplishing something."

Failure is a natural part of life, especially for people like Patricia who are accustomed to stepping further out on the limb where others fear to tread. She remembers one particular failure she experienced when she was learning the ropes.

"I used to think that when I established a baseline structure of a project, and then stepped back and let people figure it out from there, that everything would naturally work out," she explains. "But I learned the hard way that some people aren't suited to that kind of environment, and I wasn't early enough to respond and make adjustments. It didn't mean that something was wrong with me; it meant that there was something wrong with the environment that I'd created. Some people were not going to be comfortable in it. My failure was waiting for them to get to where I needed them to be, when I should have stepped in sooner. Instead, I waited for two years, and when I had the conversation with them that they weren't working out, it made them very angry. It was my fault for not having dealt with it sooner. It wasn't helpful for anyone."

As good a manager and visionary as she is in her professional life, Patricia's deepest sense of fulfillment and satisfaction comes from life with her husband and children, both of whom are in their 30s. Theirs has always been a home filled with love and laughter.

"Don and I like to travel," she says, "and we used to travel with the kids when they were growing up." She has many hobbies and interests that include visiting art museums and theaters, reading and taking walks.

"When they were younger, my kids said to their friends, 'Remember, my parents were hippies,'" she says. "What that means to our kids, I think, is that Don and I weren't those parents who had rules like you can't watch television, or, you can't go to see that movie. However, we did say that you will get good grades, you will go to college, and you will get a job. Both of my children are incredibly smart, strong-willed and good workers. They get rave reviews from everyone. Not bad for a couple of hippie parents! If you had asked me to describe one of my biggest successes, I would have told you it was my children."

Patricia's Final Thoughts

I say to women all the time not to be afraid of being strong. Don't be afraid to let people know what you know. Tell it like you see it. You don't have to hold back and pretty it up.

Women deserve an equal place at the table. Men don't have to shy away from telling it like it is or lessen the power of their convictions to appear more conservative or submissive. Why should women?

Be true to your gender. I have been, and in some ways I'm a stronger leader because of that. I have many men and women working for me, and I've observed that women are uncomfortable about being strong. We shouldn't withhold our opinions or our ideas. We shouldn't withhold what we think the world needs to do to be a better place. We should be able to be diverse. Just be true to who you are.

Bebe Ross Coker

8

Bebe Ross Coker

*"Don't let your talents and skills take you where
your character can't keep you."*

Biography

Bebe Ross Coker was born on November 16, 1935, in Jacksonville, Fla.,
where she was educated in segregated schools. She attended Morgan
State University in Baltimore, Md., and after graduation worked in
the Division of Social Services in Los Angeles, Calif. In 1960, she
moved to Wilmington, Del., where she fought to change the
segregated housing and public accommodations laws.

During the 1970s and 1980s, Bebe worked for peaceful
desegregation of schools. She was a member of the organization,
The Committee to Improve Education, and is still passionate about
equal access to quality education. She served as president of the
New Castle County Vo-Tech school board and was instrumental in
informing the community about the benefits of vocational
education. She continues to serve the community in many capacities.
Bebe writes and produces musicals and plays that teach black
history. She worked with the Wilmington Black Theater Ensemble to
present her play "Mo' Tea Miss Ann" at the DuPont Theatre Her
musical "Wake Up World," based on the thoughts of Delaware
youth, was performed at the Annenberg Center in Philadelphia.
Several of her shows were also performed in New York City.

In spring of 2013, Bebe served as a civil rights "legend" to
students at Eastside Charter School in Wilmington as part of Street
Law's Closing the Gap initiative.

Bebe has three daughters, all of whom graduated from public
schools in Wilmington.

Bebe's Story

I first met Bebe Coker at a fundraising event for the Fresh Start Scholarship Foundation. Sharon Kelly Hake, whose story I told in the first book of "Pearls," introduced us. Sharon believed that Bebe's story needed to be told, and about 30 seconds after I met Bebe, I agreed.

Bebe, a petite black woman in her 80s, is on a mission to end illiteracy. Within the first moments of our meeting, she told me the story of her recent meeting with a 40-year-old prison inmate who couldn't read. She was on fire about it—outraged. I remember what she said: "Why would you let somebody go through high school and get a diploma if they can't read? Because you just to get rid of them?"

Bebe is a devoted mother, talented writer and tireless community activist who fights what often seems like an uphill battle for the improvement of Wilmington's educational system. It is a system she believes has glaring inequities that fan the flames of criminal behavior and civil unrest exists.

Bebe was born in Jacksonville, Fla., the youngest of three children. Her parents, John Albert Ross and Cora Wood Ross, met and fell in love at Edward Waters, an African Methodist East college in Jacksonville.

Her mother, she says, was an extremely pretty and self-assured woman—not strict, but determined.

"You knew without a doubt what she wanted and what you were supposed to do," Bebe says. "We didn't grow up with a lot of whippings. But, oh! She could just look at you. You could be a mile away and still feel that look."

Bebe's father left shortly after Bebe was born to take a job at the Social Security office in Baltimore. Her mother didn't want to move north because she didn't want to leave her network of friends and family. The couple divorced.

Bebe's mother, the granddaughter of an Episcopalian minister, carried herself with dignity, a highly prized value in her household, in addition to education, courage and tenacity. She worked as a teacher and taught English and French to high school students in the public school system.

"Back in those days, you had to watch yourself in terms of how you carried yourself," says Bebe. "My mother was a lady in every sense of the word, and even when times were difficult, which they often were, she never talked about it. In African-American families, you didn't talk about what you didn't have. You just maintained and kept going."

Bebe remembers her early childhood as good. Her family was poor, but she didn't know it. There was always enough. At Christmas, she got everything she wanted.

"I knew how to set the table, and in the 1940s my mother was involved with the West Jacksonville Garden Circle," she says. "Every area in town had their own, and every year there was a competition when judges would decide which gardens were the best."

There was segregation in the south, with a separate library for black people and a separate YMCA. Even the train was segregated.

"We took the train to Baltimore every summer to see my father," Bebe says. "My mother would always make sure of it. It was called the Seaboard Airline Railroad. We always took our own lunch, because mother didn't want us to go in the dining car to sit behind the curtain. My mother had a very quiet sense of what was right and what was wrong during the Civil Rights era."

Bebe's sister, Netta, loved the library. "She just read and read," Bebe says. "She wound up being a public school librarian. She used to volunteer at the library without pay, just to be around the books. She knew the Dewey Decimal System backward and forward."

Bebe spent a lot of time at the "colored Y," where there was dancing, crafts and performing plays. It was where she discovered her love of writing and her determination to be true to herself.

"I didn't want to feel like I always had to act like a lady," she says. "There were many classy people I was expected to hang out with, but I always wanted to be around the people who were just 'regular,' so that's what I did. My mother never stopped me."

Bebe continued her love of theater and other cultural arts into her teenage years.

"In a segregated community, we created a wonderful world of our own," she says. "We wrote and produced plays, had choirs and put together art fests. In any community in the South, in the areas around universities from Atlanta to Florida, the arts thrived. I must have seen the great Marian Anderson five or six times. The sororities and fraternities brought in Roland Hays, the tenors and great plays like "Angel Street" with an entirely black company."

Bebe is a creative person by nature and would have loved to have been a full-time playwright or poet, but she says her lack of discipline kept her from pursuing it professionally. Still, she never stopped being involved.

"I wrote plays in college, and I have always written poetry," says Bebe. "I majored in sociology, though. Don't ask me why—I really have no idea. When I came to Delaware, there was a group called the Wilmington Black Theater Ensemble, which was headed by Jay Preston Powell. Every year, we put on a musical at the Grand Opera House. One of our productions was the first musical or play by a black troupe at The Playhouse Theatre in the 1970s. This show went to New York and we won the Odelco Award off-Broadway in 1982 or '83. We won the Governor's Annual Arts Award. It's a piece of Delaware silver in a glass case. Pete DuPont gave it to me."

Bebe says that she never received any restrictive messages about the role women played in society. She believes it's because of cultural differences.

"As a child, I wasn't aware that limitations even existed for women," she explains. "In our community, there were no restrictions. I always say that black women and white men are the luckiest people in the world. It's no joke—black women did what they had to do to make their way in the world. They achieved, went to school and then on to college. Black women were far better educated and faster than black men any day of the week."

Bebe's Aunt Ruth was the first Home Economics major to graduate from Carnegie Tech. Bebe's mother and another aunt graduated from the University of Pittsburgh. The men in the family skipped college and went directly to work after high school. One uncle was a Pullman car porter and another was a life-long post office employee.

Bebe went to college at Morgan State University, a historically black college in Baltimore, while the Civil Rights Movement was in full swing. She participated in many protests, both as an organizer and in the picket line.

"We protested a law that wouldn't allow blacks in public accommodations, such as the movie theater," Bebe recalls. "We protested for two weeks and we shouldn't have had to, because there's nothing the movie theater owner would have liked more than to sell us tickets and let us into the theater, which was less than a mile away from the college. But he couldn't because of the law."

Bebe and her group protested at the May Company, too, which was one of the country's largest retailers. Today, Morgan State University owns that entire area and it is now the site of a hospitality management college.

It was here that she met her husband, Larry, who became a math teacher in the Upper Merion School District. They had three daughters—Laurie, Joan and Judy, of whom you'll hear more about later—but the couple divorced after 14 years. She considers the divorce one of the greatest failures of her life.

"I was raised in an environment that encouraged black women to be strong," Bebe explains. "I watched my mother raise us by herself, and I think she did a pretty good job. I was uninformed about how to be married, because I didn't see it, and the marriages that I did see weren't that great. So I regret that our marriage didn't work. Had I known then what I know now, I would have known what to do, how to stick it out, how to change myself instead of trying to change him. You can't change anyone else. I could have done a better job. I just didn't know what to do."

After a career working for a governor and the Social Security Administration, Bebe worked as a diversity trainer for the Defense Logistics Agency in the United States Department of Defense, which employed more than 26,000 civilian and military personnel worldwide. She worked out of Philadelphia's Region 3, which serves Maryland, Virginia and New York.

"DLA was having problems keeping contracts," said Bebe. "People were doing a lot of 'white male' bashing, putting blame where it didn't belong rather than facing up to how well they were doing their own jobs. I'm a nice person, but there was a lot of BS going on, and I wasn't going to get caught up on any Kumbaya stuff. I focused on putting an end to the blame games. I wanted them to be able to respect one another for their talent and skills between 9 and 5, and after that, they were on their own."

Bebe says she's a collaborative leader. She doesn't like to be in charge at someone else's expense and she doesn't need to have a fancy title.

"If I'm supposed to be in charge of any project or program, I am going to make sure that we do what we're supposed to do," says Bebe. "We're going to do what's in the best interest of everyone concerned, and we're not going to divide and conquer. I hate it when people try to divide a group and swing people over to their side."

Bebe says she does well when communication is open, as long as people express their opposing views with respect.

"My mother always told us that you can tell someone to go to hell, but in such a nice way that they will thank you for the invitation," she says. "I've never forgotten that. There's another saying that's very profound to me: Don't let your talents take you where your character can't keep you. I have very little tolerance for the lack of integrity. Your talent is not worth a quarter if you have no character. My girls will tell you that."

Bebe is the proud mother of three accomplished women. Laurie, her first born, is a Navy captain and a nurse who works for the Center for Disease Control in Atlanta and who hopes to some day open a clinic for Alzheimer's patients. Her middle child, Joan, is a head and neck surgeon and board-certified otolaryngologist at ENT & Allergy of Delaware. Her third, Judy, was recently named CEO of the Philadelphia Convention and Visitors Bureau.

"My daughters are the best part of my life," says Bebe. "My girls are each other's right and left arm. I raised them to not allow anyone to come between them."

When not enjoying time with her children, Bebe is a tireless advocate for education and literacy.

"Education has always been very important to me," she says. "Once upon a time in Delaware, we had good schools. I don't care what anybody says. Some people say that there is an achievement gap, but I disagree. I say there is a learning opportunities gap. In a black neighborhood, you must provide the resources, materials and teachers in the schools so that the children can learn. If a teacher is worth her salt, a child can learn. There is no higher profession or any more important person than a teacher.

"I work on every community thing I can that will bring good education to our kids," she continues. "I'm old enough that I can say anything I want to, and in a recent meeting with a police committee, I told them that what we need are community centers so that kids have someplace to go and something to do. They need mentors. I asked them—'Are you fighting crime, or are you fighting criminals?' Kids need basketball, and swim teams, and drama programs. I don't get why they don't get this in this city. It's amazing to me."

Bebe's mother lived to the age of 102, and with a sharp mind and quick wit.

"One time, one of her former pupils, Albert, who was 77, came for a visit," she says. "Her 'kids' came by all the time. When we were younger, we were jealous of them and complained when they came to see Momma on weekends. 'You had her all week,' we'd say, 'and now it's *our* turn!' Anyway, my mother was in her chair and appeared to be sleeping, and Albert said something to her in French. My mother opened her eyes and said, 'That's very good, Albert, but you used the wrong tense.' We all thought that was the funniest thing and we laughed hysterically. Three months later, she was gone."

Bebe follows in her mother's footsteps, with the same reverence for education, bright spirit, wicked sense of humor a fierce devotion to her children and relentless determination to make this community a better place.

Bebe's Final Thoughts

You can't go any further than to be what you really are. That doesn't mean that you are limited. It just means you must work hard on your own abilities and not strive to be something you're naturally not. If you try and do something for the wrong reason, it isn't going to happen. Stop trying to be someone else.

Define for yourself what you see is your purpose. Purpose and passion is that thing you think about when you wake up in the morning. My passion these days is to live with a sense of urgency because I don't know if I'm going to be here tomorrow. I try to do all that I can for educational advocacy.

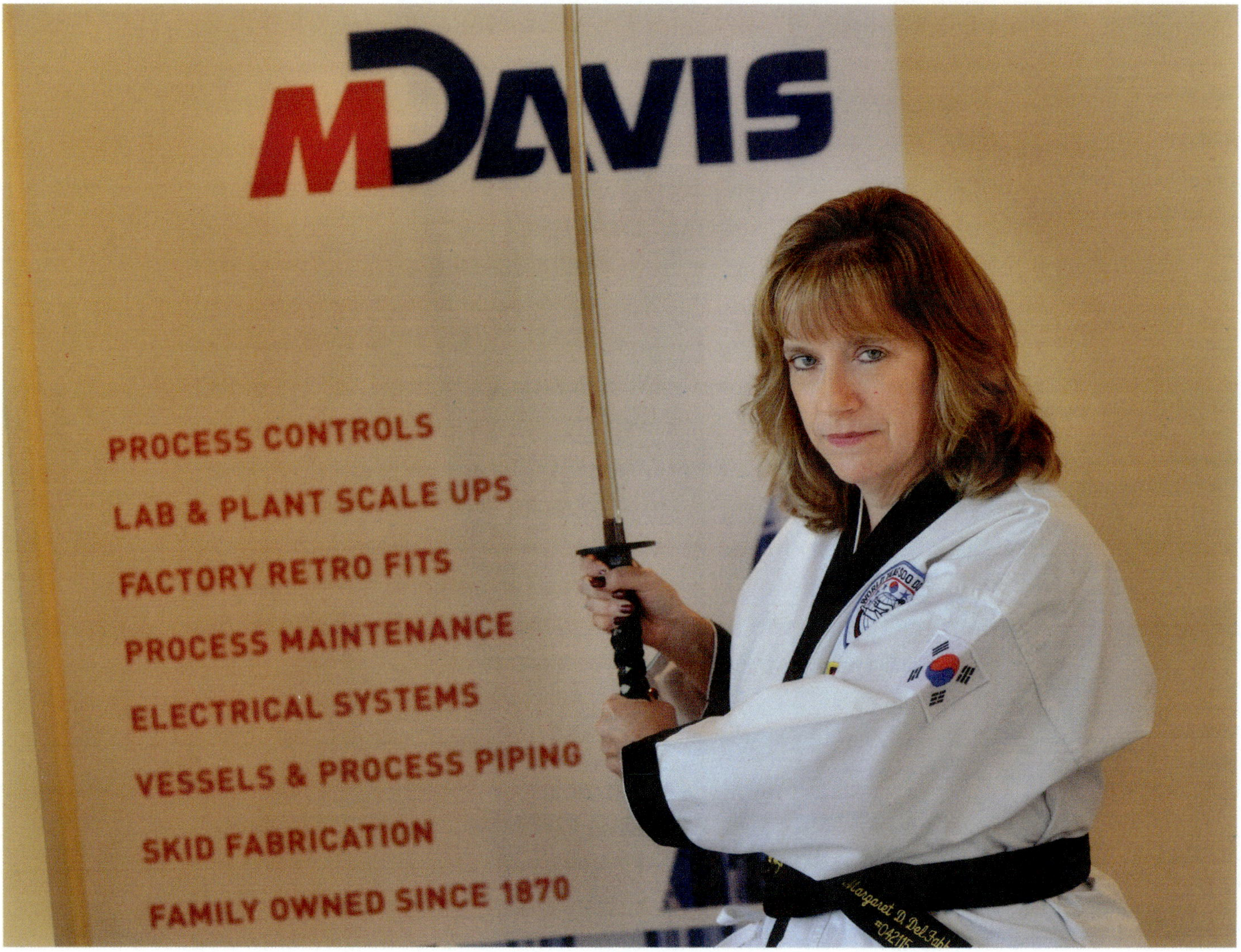

PROCESS CONTROLS

LAB & PLANT SCALE UPS

FACTORY RETRO FITS

PROCESS MAINTENANCE

ELECTRICAL SYSTEMS

VESSELS & PROCESS PIPING

SKID FABRICATION

FAMILY OWNED SINCE 1870

Peggy Delfabbro

Peggy Delfabbro

I learned early to be a coachable person ... I was open to listening to feedback so that I could apply the self-discipline and hard work it would take to be successful.

Biography

Five generations of family leadership at M. Davis & Sons is something for which CEO Peggy Davis Delfabbro, the great-great granddaughter of its founder, Edward R. Davis, is very proud. She is quick to credit the company's overall success to the strength and talent of her employees, and says they are the true sources of the company's innovation and growth.

Founded in 1870 as a tinsmith shop, M. Davis is now a full-service industrial construction company. It provides design-and-build services, fabrication, engineering and maintenance for national and international clients in the oil, gas, chemical, food and beverage, and pharmaceutical industries.

Peggy began her career at M. Davis in 1987 in its accounting department, then held various titles, including controller and treasurer. She has served on the firm's executive committee for more than two decades.

She assumed the CEO role in 2008 and works to distinguish M. Davis in the marketplace via its unwavering commitment to safety and quality. Her precise vision of M. Davis and the superior workmanship of her team has enabled the company to persevere during economically troubled times.

A graduate of the University of Delaware with a bachelor's in business administration, Peggy is an active member of the Women's Business Enterprise National Council PA-DE-SNJ chapter, including its Envoy program. She also served as a local chapter treasurer for the National Association of Women in Construction.

A socially concerned business leader, Peggy financially supports several community programs.

Peggy's Story

A visit to a large industrial construction site or fabrication facility is an assault on the senses, with its huge steel girders, showers of hot sparks, deafening clanks and manly shouts. There are hard hats, safety glasses, and skilled employees with calloused hands. There are concrete slabs, miles of electrical wire and sophisticated machinery. Journeyman and apprentice workers boast multiple capabilities. Multi-million dollar projects are executed flawlessly nationwide for some of the world's most powerful companies.

The leader in charge of the behemoth called M. Davis & Sons, Inc., a 145-year, multi-generational industrial construction company (and a tour de force in Wilmington) is not whom one would expect. You'd think it would be a man, right? An eldest son, perhaps, who reports to the office in a suit and tie, but by day's end has his sleeves rolled up, and is poring over complex architectural drawings with other men who wear hard hats, flannel and sturdy work boots. It's right out of central casting.

But you'd be mistaken.

This boss is a petite woman with long blonde hair who wears stylish suits. She's down-to-earth and friendly. She could never compete on her company's football team (if there was one), but it doesn't matter. Being the CEO of M. Davis & Sons and earning the respect of its employees, clients and community comes as naturally to Peggy Delfabbro as breathing. It's in her blood.

Born in Wilmington, Del., Peggy is the youngest of two daughters born to Charles and Helen Davis. Charles, the fourth Davis family member to take the helm at M. Davis & Sons, is credited with the dramatic expansion of the company's expertise, services and client growth. Helen, born into a well-to-do Mississippi family, brought to the Davis household an air of southern gentility and charm. Her father was a chemist at Hercules, Inc., a DuPont spin-off known for its production of gunpowder and other explosives.

"Mom wasn't a dainty Southern belle, however," says Peggy. "She could be pretty down-to-earth as well. She's a big sports fan, so while I was growing up, we watched a lot of ice hockey."

Peggy's mother and grandmother managed the company's payroll. M. Davis & Sons was much smaller at the time, and had just six full-time employees. "I still have some of the original hand-written ledgers," Peggy says. "Since both women were involved in the business while juggling life at home, it never occurred to me that our life was out of the ordinary with two working women in the family."

Peggy describes the influence her mother and grandmother had on the business as "quietly powerful."

"I remember when my family got together for discussions regarding the best interests of the company," Peggy says, "and though my mother and grandmother weren't as vocal, their influences were very strong. I was close with my grandmother, and I watched her closely. She made people feel good about themselves. The guys in the shop loved and respected her, but she wasn't a pushover. My mother was the same way."

Peggy's father, now 79, was influential as well, in terms of how his daughter would end up viewing the world. He still attends the company's strategic planning meetings, and Peggy often feels as if a stern but loving professor is visiting her.

"*Uh-oh, here he comes*, I'll think," says Peggy, "because he likes to give me a list of things I should do to solve a particular problem. I usually say, 'Yes, Dad, I've already done that. I've already done that, too.' We think alike most of the time, so I'm sure the solutions I've come up with have a bit of both of us in them."

Peggy is passionate about cultivating a positive workplace culture, a virtue she says was passed along to her by her father.

"He always used to say that M. Davis is nothing without our great team of people," she says. "We wouldn't have a business without them. The work we do here is difficult, and there are days when people labor long and hard, so our tradition is to share the rewards of whatever profits are there. Our philosophy is to reinvest in the business and reward the people who work here. We want them to have the best tools and resources, and I think they know and appreciate that."

Peggy's sister, Carolyn, was born severely disabled, and her parents made the difficult decision to move her to a place that could provide proper care. They made another difficult but courageous decision when they tried to have more children, and Peggy came along.

"Being a parent now, I can appreciate how difficult that decision must have been for them," says Peggy. "It was a huge risk. Looking back, I can see that the experience grounded us as a family. I learned at an early age that life and health shouldn't be taken for granted. It matured me, in a way."

Peggy was painfully shy as a young girl. She remembers making presentations in high school and college and being barely audible. "It's hard to imagine now, with all the public speaking that I do," she says. "I don't remember specifically when this changed—I'm still a bit on the shy side—but I think something was awakened in me over time, after I became the CEO. I realized that being a CEO changed the way people looked at me. Out of necessity, I had to take on a larger leadership persona. I'm grateful for the support I received from the women's business community along the way. Their guidance and education really helped me."

As a teenager, Peggy had little time to get into trouble. She attended school, worked at the business, and pursued her dream of becoming a figure skating champion.

"I got up at 4:30 a.m. so that I could get ice time at the Skating Club of Wilmington," says Peggy. "After that, I'd go to school, and then report to M. Davis to work. If I could, I'd squeeze in some extra time skating. My days were jam-packed."

But she loved it. There were many Olympic-level skaters in Wilmington, and Peggy reveled in their presence. She continued to skate for years as an adult, but was forced to give up the sport after a back injury affected her balance.

"My kids were taking karate classes while I was still skating," Peggy says, "and they'd say, 'C'mon, Mom, you've got to try it!' I told them I would if I ever gave up skating. So when that fateful day arrived, my kids held me to my word. And you know what? I really liked it. It was strange to switch from a girlie sport with sequins and leotards to one that was completely opposite, but I found it to be a great stress reliever. It's like taking a mental vacation. I just earned my third-degree black belt."

The karate she's learning is called Tang Soo Do, a Korean martial arts discipline that teaches movement, weapons, sparring, self-defense, knife-defense and other forms of physical combat. I told Peggy to remind me never to tick her off.

"My boys, Jeremy and Zachary (18 and 21, respectively) say to people, 'Watch out! Don't mess with her—she'll put you in a head lock,'" Peggy says.

Peggy graduated from the University of Delaware with a bachelor's in business administration with a concentration in operations management. She particularly enjoyed the marketing and sales courses. She's a self-described face-to-face people person, as opposed to someone who sits in front of a computer all day.

"I like going to the job site and actually seeing what's going on, rather than having to look at pieces of paper and review numbers," she says. "I learned that from my dad. When I was a kid, dad would say after dinner, 'I need to go check out a job site. Want to go with me?' We'd put on our work boots and take a ride."

She also remembers the lessons her grandfather taught her, like to be careful around sheet metal because it was sharp, or to avoid looking at men who were welding because of the potential of developing welder flash, an eye condition caused by exposure of insufficiently protected eyes to ultraviolet rays or artificial light sources.

"The most important thing about visiting a site is to see how our guys are doing and whether they're all right," adds Peggy. "I want to see the conditions they're working in, what progress they've made, and to ensure that all requirements are being met. I can't just sit in my office to get that kind of insight."

I tried to picture petite Peggy visiting a northern New Jersey construction site and wondered how she held her own in such a traditionally male environment. She said she did not experience much gender discrimination, and that surprised me.

"I have had a man or two challenge me to test my competence or knowledge," she says, "but I've handled it quickly and effectively. We did a project a couple of years ago at a site I'd never seen. It was one of the biggest jobs we'd ever done. I made plans to visit the site at least once per month, if not more. At the first meeting, one of the members of the client team, a man, asked me a challenging question, almost impertinently, and I heard the men on my team gasp in alarm. I don't remember the question or how I answered it, but I remember coming right back at him and putting him in his place without making a scene. After that, everything went very smoothly.

Every once in a while, a man tests me. It happens. But I always nip it in the bud."

Peggy was blessed with many mentors throughout her life. Her parents and grandparents were the first of many, and she gives special credit to her figure skating and karate coaches.

"I learned early to be a coachable person, and to have a positive view about criticism," says Peggy. "In skating, I wasn't a good jumper, but I was open to listening to feedback so that I could apply the self-discipline and hard work it would take to be successful.

"In the beginning of my karate adventures, I told all of my instructors to be brutally honest with me," she adds. "Since I couldn't skate any more, I wanted to be the best I could in my new sport. I wanted to excel at tournaments, and I always told my coaches, 'Be brutally honest with me. Don't pull any punches—coach me!'"

Another favorite mentor for Peggy is Geri Swift, president of the PA-DE-SNJ chapter of the Women's Business Enterprise Council (WBENC).

"She's been a tremendous role model for me," says Peggy. "She encourages me to take leadership roles and gives me opportunities to speak in front of large groups of people. My confidence has grown tenfold because of her."

Peggy worked at M. Davis throughout her college years. "I did whatever needed to be done in the office—answer phones, take tool inventories—but I wasn't a very good typist," she says.

After college she accepted a job at one of M. Davis's customers and held that position for four years. When Peggy's father asked her to work for the family-owned company as a supervisor in its accounting department, she accepted, but remembers this career phase as being her most difficult.

"I had never been a supervisor before," she explains. "On top of that, I was the boss's daughter. The staff didn't know me. I'd been gone for four years and many employees had come on board since then. I fumbled my way through it. I had no idea how to manage staff, and I was afraid to confront problems. I hated letting people go, even if the reasons were sound. I didn't even know what a W---2 form was. But I persevered, just as I did as a figure skater who couldn't jump, and eventually, I found my stride."

One of Peggy's first initiatives was to computerize the accounting department. "I was okay with making process improvements," she says, "but the people part of it has never been easy for me. Even today there are situations with personnel that throw me. I always ask myself what I could have done to make that person be more successful. Could I have made our expectations easier to understand? Are they having difficulties with the job? I prefer to get to the bottom of their challenges, and give them a chance to fix things. If the situation doesn't get better, then at least I've done the decent thing by extending to them additional opportunities. I've learned to be comfortable with that."

Peggy met her husband, Adrian Delfabbro, through a college friend while attending the University of Delaware. A skilled auto mechanic, Adrian was in business with his brothers and had also worked in his father's sign shop. After they married, they had two sons, and then decided that one of them needed to say home with the kids. Daycare expenses were cost prohibitive, and they didn't want the boys to miss out on anything. Because Peggy's responsibilities at M. Davis were expanding and it seemed likely that she would soon lead the company, Adrian took on the role of stay-at-home dad.

"He was wonderful," Peggy says. "And it was the perfect solution for us. Now that the boys are grown and fairly self sufficient, we decided to adopt a couple of rescue dogs—puppies at that. It kind of messes things up, having a couple of baby dogs running around, but they're so cute and we're dealing with it."

I asked Peggy whether she was grooming her sons to take over the business.

"Zachary spent a summer working in the shop," she says, "and we decided it's really not his thing. He's more science-oriented, and very interested in animal behavior. He works at Faithful Friends (a Delaware-based, no-kill animal shelter) and loves it. He's not sure what kind of career this passion will morph into, but he's fascinated with learning about how dogs think and react."

Jeremy, she continues, "just spent his second summer working in the shop, and knock wood, he really likes it. He is very mechanically inclined. I used to bring home reports of the company's open jobs. At 13, he'd pore over them and say things like, 'Well, that job's not going well.' He is also very responsible with his money. He's only 17, but we'll see."

Peggy is a believer and supporter of Delaware's vocational technical education system. She and several M. Davis colleagues visit various vo---tech schools and share their experiences with students. "We provide tools, we donate materials and we hire their co---op students," she says. "We have eight to 10 students join us every summer on a full---time basis. During the school year, they alternate going to school for two weeks then working with us for two weeks. If they do a good job, we invite them to join us permanently. These students walk out of high school with full-time jobs and benefits. Next, we enter them into the apprenticeship program, and four years later, they have earned their journeymen papers, which, in my opinion, is every bit as valuable as a college degree. Not everyone can afford to go to college. It's a joy for me to be able to give back this way."

In addition to the numerous other organizations supported by M. Davis & Sons, Peggy also supports the Delaware Military Academy, where her two sons attended school. "I love the idea of discipline that they instill there," says Peggy, "and that they keep the school small. It was a great school for my kids."

Peggy's Final Thoughts

One of the biggest pieces of advice Peggy shares with other women is to have a plan.

"I've seen many women flounder because they didn't have a plan," she says, adding that for years she's been volunteering for groups who help and support female business owners. "My advice is to really think through your product or service. Take a little extra time to think everything through before you take that big leap. Make sure you're organized and have a clear direction. You need to do lots of research. Be sure you understand what it will take to be successful in your chosen endeavor. Once you have a good plan, everything else will fall into place. I can talk about this: Our company has survived for 145 years because our founders and predecessors laid out their plans for the future very carefully."

Roxane Ferguson
with family-Alexis (left), **Kevin** *and* **Zachery**

Roxane Ferguson

"Change offers you opportunities that you've yet to imagine."

Biography

Roxane Ferguson is the executive director of the Middletown Area Chamber of Commerce. She has also served as the executive director of the Southern Chester County Chamber of Commerce; marketing director for Diamond Technologies; director of sales, membership and marketing for the Delaware Better Business Bureau; vice president of Wachovia Bank, and is a Delaware-licensed Realtor.

She graduated magna cum laude from Wesley College, earning a bachelor of science degree in business administration, and a summa cum laude graduate of Wilmington University, where she earned a master's in organizational leadership.

With 25 years of marketing, technology and management experience, Roxane has facilitated many changes for the organizations she has represented. Her most recent project is the creation of a business incubator and collaborative workspace in Middletown, Del., the first of its kind in the region.

In addition, Roxane serves as a board member for the MOT Senior Center; the district public relations chair for Rotary International, and an adjunct professor at Longwood Gardens. This sports enthusiast is an active member of the Delaware Press Association and enjoys frequent visits to the Poconos and Cape Henlopen.

Roxane resides in Middletown, Del., with her husband, Kevin, and their children, Alexis and Zachery.

Roxane's Story

Roxane likes to connect people to each other and makes herself available to others as well. Now that she and I have become better acquainted, I can understand her passion for those connections.

She's a mover and shaker of the first order; someone who delights in making good things happen. In challenging times, she's at the forefront, facing down the dragon and pushing for what's right. Roxane always has a smile on her face. This is perhaps the biggest reason I wanted to include her in "Pearls."

Small business owners and doe-eyed entrepreneurs, who are people with big dreams and a tough row to hoe, surround Roxane all day. They need opportunities for growth, education and moral support to keep them in the game—and to remember why they jumped on this crazy ride in the first place. Roxane has the spirit and leadership skills to help them stay true to their visions, step into their power, and to simply keep smiling.

She was born at Scared Heart Hospital in Chester, Pa. to a woman she's never met. It doesn't matter, because five days later, Agnes and Paul Petro, a couple unable to have children of their own, adopted Roxane and raised her in a happy home.

"My adoptive mom was an amazing woman," says Roxane. "She was proud to be a coal miner's daughter. She grew up in Centralia, which is a mine fire town. She loved children."

Three years after adopting Roxane, Agnes and Paul adopted another girl, Nicole, and when Agnes turned 40, she became pregnant with Roxane's little brother, Brent.

"There was a 10-year difference between Brent and me, and because he didn't have siblings closer in age, my mother opened a home-based daycare center," Roxane says. "Mom took care of children of all races. We'd all do each other's hair and learn about diversity. It was amazing. My brother made many good friends."

Roxane describes her adoptive father as "really cool." He once drove race cars for Penske, and for a time, trained elephants for Ringling Brothers—an experience loaded with colorful stories that Roxane is reluctant to tell. An Air Force veteran, Paul was a mechanical engineer who for many years worked for Scott Paper in

Philadelphia. Later, he worked for DuPont until he was 82, and before a hip replacement and a brain injury from a fall ended his ability to drive.

"Mom passed away three years ago, so Dad is on his own," says Roxane, her eyes glowing with affection. "My sister and I visit him often."

"He has the most beautiful handwriting," she continues. "He puts an envelope underneath the paper so that his sentences run perfectly across the page. He tells me that back in the day they didn't have lined paper. I tell my kids to pay attention to their Pop-Pop, and also to my husband's mother, Nannie, who's 80, because of all the things they can learn about how the world used to be."

Roxane's father was a strong disciplinarian and a devoted father. Roxane credits him with having shaped her penchant for community service.

"He showed me by example that doing little things can make a big difference," explains Roxane. "At the age of seven, I began having backyard fairs. I was a party planner even then! My father helped me make the promotional posters to reach out to the neighborhood parents. Afterward we'd take all of the money we earned and donated it to the Phillies charities."

Roxane says she was ornery as a child, a tomboy who liked to ride bikes, build ramps and play sports. "I had a girlie side, too," she says. "I was a majorette, and I liked getting dressed up. I played the flute because Mom always encouraged us to try everything. I encourage my children to try musical things, too. I even married a musician!"

Roxane describes her 16th as the most influential year of her life; one that taught her that change was unavoidable, inevitable, sometimes painful, but often exhilarating. This was the year her father got her a 1975 Camaro, but also the year she was ripped away from her comfortable childhood life in New Castle, Del.

"My father's No. 1 ambition as a father was keeping us safe," she explains. "He wanted me in a car that would allow me to be able to drive away from unsafe situations if I needed to. The Camaro was built of solid metal, with serious upgrades my father had installed himself. For example, he hooked up the blinkers so that they'd flash when the fuel gauge showed I was low on gas."

At the end of her junior year in high school, Paul accepted a job at Merck and moved the family to Bloomsburg, Pa. The then-teenaged Roxane was devastated and acted out her anger around the house.

"I was a terror on wheels," she says. "I was upset because I had to leave all my friends and my boyfriend behind. I cried and sulked all summer. I think my mom was waiting for my head to spin all the way around. I couldn't understand how they could do such a terrible thing to me, moving me to a place where cow-tipping was a favorite pastime."

However, true to her outgoing, happy nature, Roxane quickly adjusted and in her senior year got voted to the homecoming court; made the varsity field hockey team; and was assumed to be cool because she came from the city and drove a tricked-out Camaro. Life improved in many ways, despite her former belief that she'd been exiled to Hicksville and doomed to teenage purgatory.

"We had a lot of relatives up there, so it wasn't so bad," Roxane explains. "I got a job at a place called Knoebel's Grove, a wonderful amusement resort. I learned quite a bit about horticulture there. Our softball team made division championships, and I was Mardi Gras queen. It was a phenomenal year."

Roxane attended Bloomsburg University for a year, and then went to Hawaii to study sociology at Brigham Young University. When her father accepted a new position at DuPont and moved the family back to Delaware, Roxane moved home and took a job at CoreStates Bank. At 21, she married her high school sweetheart, but the marriage ended after a year-and-a-half.

"We'll always be close," she says, "I love his family, and my cousin married his brother. But neither of us were ready for that kind of commitment."

At 30, she married Kevin Ferguson, and it stuck. They've been together for 25 years and have two children. She'd been working at CoreStates for 11 years and had regularly been promoted, but she suspected her options for rising further up the ladder were limited because she hadn't yet earned a college degree.

"Without a degree I couldn't even get an interview," Roxane says, "so I announced to my husband that I was going back to college. I took a job at DuPont, where they had a preschool, then took classes at Wesley College. I did really well there: got my bachelor's in business administration—magna cum laude—and was inducted into the Alpha Chi Honor Society.

Because her husband had a contracting business, Roxane developed an intimate knowledge of the construction and real estate industries, which helped her get a job at Ryan Homes. The job was fun, but it demanded long, irregular hours, and as the mother of two small children, she looked for other options.

"I was blessed enough to get a job at the Better Business Bureau," she says. "I met a lot of really great people there. I got to travel all around the state, work with small businesses and attend chamber events. I developed a passion for business—every little bit of it: how it operates; the courage and determination it takes; the challenges of longevity and scalability. I wanted more!"

She got more by earning a master's in organizational leadership at Wilmington University. True to Roxane's self-described "blonde logic" and an educational journey that moved one way and then the other, she earned that graduate degree with honors.

"First, I had to figure out how to pay for the tuition," Roxane says. "So I got a job with an IT firm that reimbursed me for the costs. Halfway through my program, the economy took a hit and the firm downsized me, which opened up the opportunity for me to become the executive director for the Southern Chester County Chamber of Commerce. I worked there for two years, creating their first strategic plan, and finished up my master's, summa cum laude."

Upon graduation, Roxane studied for, and earned, her real estate license. Why? "Sh*ts and giggles," she says. She also has a bartending license.

"I never **wanted to be in the position I was in after 10 years of banking and not having been able to find a decent job without a college degree,"** says Roxane. **"I saw the value in having a diverse background and I wanted to improve my leadership skills in a diverse range of industries."**

She had been downsized several times in her life, but was determined to make the best of it.

"Instead of getting upset about these job losses, wondering what I'd done to deserve the misfortune, I decided to roll with the change rather than be rolled over by it," she says. "Where you come out and where you land, you never know, and if you can see the gift in that, then every day is Christmas. In banking I'd been laid off, then rehired several times, but I found a way to enjoy it nevertheless. I didn't have children yet, so I'd take the severance and live at the beach for a year!"

Impressed with the strategic plan she'd created for the Southern Chester County Chamber, Roxane was invited to be an adjunct professor at Longwood Gardens. She's held that position for seven years.

"They have a business management component in their professional gardener program, which I teach," she says. "I love to teach and I love to learn. I believe that in life, we're never *not* learning. If you open your mind, there's so much you can gain from every experience."

Roxane is a "get it done" kind of person. She has been described as a "master of the spinning plates," someone who is able to handle several tasks at once, including balancing her home and professional lives.

"An important skill I've developed over the years was how to say no, and it's powerful," says Roxane. "I've also learned to handle challenges head on. For example, if one of my kids was being bullied, I'd look into it, and if I saw a way to effect positive change in the system and address the problem, I'd go for it."

One time, she took gender discrimination by the horns and wrestled with it. She took a police officer to court who, Roxane believed, gave her a ticket because she was female.

"I didn't win the case," Roxane says, "but the female judge said she wishes she could have done more. She saw to it that the officer was penalized in other ways. I'd done everything I could, and I felt satisfied that I had stood up for my rights. We all need to do that when injustice happens. I admire the women who lobby for equal status in the workplace. It takes courage.

"We owe it to ourselves to influence change whenever we can," she continues. "When I was in banking and there more layoffs, we had to do something called forced ranking. This is when you have to take a look at all of your employees and rank them as to who's going to have a job and who is not. And, I had to do it even though I knew

I was going to be one of the people to lose her job! The problem was, these rankings were made subjectively. There were no guidelines.

Roxane went to the other managers and said they needed to have a process in place. "They can't just go in there willy-nilly and randomly take away people's livelihoods," she says.

"We worked together to develop a set of core values (that other businesses now use as their core values), and a system that ensured every single staff member received fair consideration and not be discriminated against based on their age, gender, whether they liked sports and other such personal judgments," she says.

Roxane describes her leadership style as charismatic. "I want people to find the best in themselves," she explains, "and I love connecting people. We're not islands, and the more people we connect with, the more help we each have on our journey."

For fun, Roxane loves to dance, and it's fortunate she married a musician because she gets plenty of opportunities to do her thing.

"I love to do anything that involves my family," she says. "We have a house in the Poconos, and we love to ski. There's a story about our Pocono house that involves a renter, cigar, fire, police standoff and hand grenades. Crazy stuff! I always say, 'go big, or go home.' We're rebuilding. We also love Cape Henlopen. We pile into the car—kids, dog, grill—stop at Grottos and just hang out at the beach all day."

Roxane and her husband recently discussed plans for the future, and they made a bucket list, most of which includes traveling and spending time with their kids.

"My daughter, Alexis, graduates from high school in 2017, and we'll be celebrating our 20th anniversary that year," says Roxane, "so we're going to take the kids to Hawaii for two weeks. I'll be able to show them where I went to college. My daughter deserves a treat. She's in the Air Force R.O.T.C., the Civil Air Patrol; has lettered in four sports, and works at Chick-Fil-A. She would like to go into the military, become an attorney, and get into the JAG Corps. We're so proud of her."

When their son, Zachary, graduates, the family will travel to England and Scotland, where her husband's family is from. Zach will love that, says Roxane, because he's fascinated by the family's history.

"And then, when both of the kids are in college, we're going to sell the house and I'm going back to school for my doctorate," Roxane says. "My husband wants to earn a bachelor's, and we'll be able to tell people we went to college together. I'm hoping we can get a fellowship and live on campus. That'll be such fun!"

Roxane's biggest advice to women is to get involved in something they're passionate about.

"If you listen to your passion, you can be an entrepreneur and do something that you really love," she says. "If you're trying to identify your passion, get involved in things you're interested in and see where that leads you. Sometimes it's good to work in an area you're interested in before you commit to something. Being a temp allows you to try different things, but be careful. You don't want to be a temp so that the company can try *you* on for size. It's the other way around. You should be checking *them* out. You want to see what kind of culture they have and what kinds of benefits they offer.

"Keep in mind that in today's work environment, everyone can expect to have seven to 10 jobs during their career," she adds. "It's not like my father's time, when people worked at the same company for decades. Definitely consider joining your local chamber of commerce. They'll be able to provide many resources that will help you professionally, such as S.C.O.R.E. and the Small Business Administration. There's usually someone like me on staff who loves helping people connect."

Roxane's Final Thoughts

When I became pregnant with my daughter, my adoptive mom wanted me to try to find my birth mother so that we could track down her medical records. We wanted to know whether there were any hereditary medical conditions I needed to be aware of.

I truly wasn't interested in finding her, except for one reason—she might be Goldie Hawn. All my life I've been told I look exactly like her. Was it possible she and Kurt Russell were my biological parents?

When my parents adopted me, they'd been told that my birth mother, having believed her husband had been killed in Vietnam, had an affair and became pregnant. During the pregnancy, she learned her husband was coming home, so she gave me up for adoption. Somewhere out there, I have half brothers and sisters I've never met.

Elizabeth Platt, a woman who came from an influential Philadelphia family (Platt Bridge), helped my parents with the adoption. My middle name is Elizabeth, in honor of her.

But my point is this: the woman who adopted me, who to me is my real mother, is the most amazing, wonderful, witty mother anyone could ever have. One day, when I was at the bus stop, the kids teased me about being adopted. My mother comforted me, dried my tears and gave me the best comeback ever.

The next day at the bus stop, when the kids taunted me, I said, "You know, your parents *had* to take you. I was *chosen*."

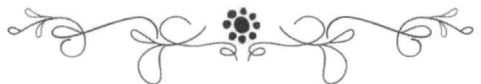

Pat Forester

Pat Forester

Building a business takes a lot of determination, passion and the desire to do good work. I have never seen anyone build a successful business on money alone.

Biography

Pat Forester is a legend in Delaware. Active in both the marketing and public relations fields since 1970, she was one of few women in management positions in what was then a male-dominated industry. She started her career in Philadelphia as a research specialist, and in 1977, joined the Gauge Corporation in Wilmington, Del., as lead account executive and public relations counsel for numerous Delaware government agencies, including the Delaware Economic Development Office, Delaware Department of Transportation, Delaware Division of Incorporations, Delaware River & Bay Authority, and the Port of Wilmington.

Gauge Corporation also specialized in association management services, a division that allowed Pat to serve as executive director of the American Institute of Architects (Delaware Chapter), the Consulting Engineers Council of Delaware, and the Port of Wilmington Maritime Society. She was responsible for planning and managing myriad special events. Gauge's Center for Social Marketing division focused on working with the nonprofit sector, and Pat led a team that created several community-focused programs for the Delaware Division of Health & Social Services that still thrive today. When the firm's owner and Pat's mentor, Edwin Golin, retired in 1990, Pat founded Forester & Company and continued working with many of the same clients while also adding new projects. She sold the firm in 2004. A supporter of the Fresh Start Scholarship Foundation, Pat founded the Blue Hen Wonder Women, a supportive network of Delaware women that has more than 100 members.

Although she is proud of her success, Pat's most significant achievement is raising five sons with her husband Jerry Forester, who passed away in 2008.

Pat's Story

She has been described as one of Delaware's most prominent marketing strategists, a networking queen and a whirlwind of positivity. I'd like to add that Pat Forester is the person you should sit next to at stuffy dinner parties.

Pat strikes me as a woman who lives beyond boundaries: unhindered by rules, but able to abide by them if necessary. She would be equally comfortable in a smoke-filled speakeasy crammed with mobsters as she would in the art deco penthouse suite of a foreign diplomat. She's an "unsinkable Molly Brown" for Delawareans.

I am one of hundreds of Delawareans who has known Pat for years. The two of us form a mutual admiration society. She makes everyone—including me—feel valued and special. That's her gift.

Given her jolly temperament, she's prone to wily winks, gentle elbow jabs and sly side-to-side glances. And when she does any of those things—if you're lucky enough to be near her—you get the feeling she's about to tell you a deliciously naughty secret. She's inclusive. She is the embodiment of one of Maya Angelou's most famous quotes: *At the end of the day, people won't remember what you said, or what you did, but how you made them feel.* Simply put, Pat makes me feel happy. I'm lucky to know her.

The eldest of three siblings, Pat was born in the Highland Gardens neighborhood of Chester, Pa. Her family was a happy one, and their starter home was purchased on the GI bill after her father returned home from serving in World War II.

"It was a great, safe neighborhood," Pat says. "Everybody knew and looked out for each other. We kids could go and play several blocks away, but if we did something wrong, someone would call our parents and tell on us. There was a strong sense of community, with neighbors looking out for one another."

Pat idolized her father, Bill Blanton, and he was her first mentor. He had a well-developed sense of responsibility and endured the difficulties and uncertainties of life with a smile. He also had a fierce determination to succeed.

"Dad was 12 when his father died," says Pat, "and he quit school at 16 to help support his four younger siblings. For one job, when he was still a height-challenged 16-year-old, he put blocks in his shoes to appear taller so he could get hired to drive a tractor trailer from Chester to Washington, D.C."

He also roller-skated professionally with his sister Jeanette, and they travelled the east coast. He met Pat's mother Madeline (also called Pat) at the Great Leopard Skating Rink in Chester and gave her skating lessons.

"She fell for him," says Pat. "Even though he appeared tough and athletic, he was actually very graceful — and an excellent skater."

Shortly after they married, Bill was sent overseas to serve in World War II. Patricia (Pat), who was named in honor of St. Patrick's Day, was born when Bill returned home four years later. The next three years would bring another daughter Linda, then a son, Bill.

"My father worked at Westinghouse for nearly his entire career," says Pat. "We had very little at times, mostly when the workers went on strike for months, but we kids never knew that. My father would make ends meet by working at nearby Fetterman's Orchards. In fact, the fruit trees he grew in our backyard were his pride and joy. He and my mother canned all of the fruit."

Pat's mother passed away in 2014 at 94. She remembers her as an extremely talented woman who seemed to do everything well. "She would go to a dress shop, examine a dress she liked, and then make it without a pattern," Pat says. "She made the recital costumes for all the schoolchildren. I'd go to school in the morning, and when I'd come home for lunch, there would be 50 handmade snowflake or gingerbread man costumes in all different sizes."

Pat attended the Resurrection of Our Lord grammar school in Chester, Pa., and then in 1965, graduated from Notre Dame High School in Moylan, Pa. She describes herself as an overachiever who took both the commercial and secretarial tracks but no electives. She was also a Catholic Scout, earning the Marian Award, the Catholic Scout's highest honor, the equivalent of an Eagle Scout award. In addition, she was selected from more than 150 girl scouts to recite the American Creed at the 100th Anniversary of Delaware County event.

"Actually, 20 of us started out working toward the Marian Award, but only three of us finished. If I make up my mind that I'm going to do something, I do it."

She credits her parents for that grit and tenacity. And while she was proud to be a Blanton, there were drawbacks. "My father coached the baseball team," she says, "and although girls weren't permitted to play then, I was allowed to keep score and help with batting practice. All the kids on the team were boys my age, and eventually I noticed that none of them ever asked me out on dates. My friends were dating like crazy, but I wasn't. And then it finally dawned on me: I was Coach Blanton's daughter. No one had the nerve!"

It never occurred to Pat that she'd do anything different than her female peers were doing. Yet in the months that followed her high school graduation, weddings occurred every weekend. "I didn't get married until I was 20," she says. "It sounds silly now, but back then, 20 was pushing it."

While her high school friends were getting hitched, Pat got a job in the human resources and marketing department at the nearby Commonwealth Land Title Insurance Company, where she met John McClain. He would become her second mentor.

"John taught me how to treat people and how to get the job done," Pat says. "He was a real Irishman — very fond of the drink — but he saw something in me and said I'd be good in the marketing business. And because of him, I had some wonderful opportunities to learn, grow and succeed."

The company had a branch in Media, Pa. When it became short-- staffed, John sent Pat to fill in. That's where she met a title clerk named Jerry Forester. She calls him the "yin to her yang," but at the beginning of their relationship, he got her in very serious trouble with her parents.

"I was dating someone else when I met Jerry," Pat says. "One day, Jerry asked whether I'd go with him to an office function, but I had already planned to attend a family reunion with my other boyfriend. Besides, I wasn't sure I liked the idea of going out with someone I worked with. It was a small office, and I was afraid it would be awkward. But I liked Jerry, so I reasoned that if I timed it right, I could do both things and have two dates. Well, I timed it wrong."

Her boyfriend said he'd pick her up at 7 p.m., but she forgot and didn't check her watch until 7:30. "I decided to stay out with Jerry, and didn't get home until midnight," says Pat. "When I snuck quietly in the door so as to not wake my parents, I noticed my boyfriend sitting on the living room sofa flanked by mom and dad. My parents were furious with me for having broken my commitment to him. It was the worst night of my life. But Jerry laughed hysterically about it later. As it turns out, he became the love of my life."

They married and had five sons, all successful adults now. Sadly, Jerry died in 2008 of Parkinson's disease, but also suffered from dementia, prostate cancer and bladder failure. He was 69.

When Pat talked about losing Jerry, there was a short pause in our conversation. And for a moment, she lost her spark. She drifted to a different place. Then, just as suddenly, she was back, alert and full of life.

"When I was pregnant with my first son," she says, "I had to leave my job at Commonwealth. That's the way it was in the 1960s, but I always managed to stay busy doing entrepreneurial kinds of things. Jerry had a friend whose wife had started a market research business. Her name was Joan Malarkey. She let me help her with various market research projects, and I loved it."

One of the first projects they worked on together was test marketing a new detergent — the first detergent with added fabric softener. "Our job was to recruit 100 people to find the ones who could rave on camera about the product," Pat recalls. "We'd interview 10 people every 10 minutes at the Presidential Hotel in Philadelphia, making brief infomercials. The client paid us $15 per person plus expenses, which was a lot of money back then."

Pat had a baby nearly two weeks later, after the project ended. But things still needed to be communicated. She says she asked the other women in the ward to make phone calls on behalf of a client. "I told you I was an entrepreneur," she says.

Another of Pat's projects involved the Southeastern Pennsylvania Transportation Authority, known regionally as SEPTA. "We'd hold clipboards and visit different stations," she says, "counting the passengers as they got on and off the buses or trains. SEPTA was exploring whether they should expand or limit service in certain areas."

Meanwhile, Jerry's career was progressing, and the young parents moved to Delaware to pursue a business opportunity. When Pat's younger sons entered kindergarten, she was ready for a new challenge. As it happened, her neighbor told her about a small marketing company that needed help and had been in business for 25 years. Its staff had never been expanded beyond the owner and his female business partner. But they were securing huge accounts nevertheless.

"When they landed the Delaware Department of Transportation as a client, they needed support with marketing research and production," says Pat. "A short time later, the Delaware River and Bay Authority signed up, then the Delaware Transport Corporation, known as DART, then the Delaware Economic Development Office. It was a true ground-floor opportunity for me."

Ed Golin, its owner, would become Pat's third and most influential mentor. She's never forgotten her first meeting with him. "I walked into his office for an interview on a Friday afternoon and walked out with a huge pile of paper," she says. "Ed was struggling with a proposal, and because he'd done his research, he knew I'd worked with SEPTA and could easily write it. So I did." Two weeks later, they landed the client.

Pat's war stories about working with Ed are star-studded, racy and peppered with achievements. There were several "firsts" and behind-the-scenes views of people who held politically powerful positions in the '80s and '90s. Their massive client base boasted the largest government agencies, the most influential associations — and even had a publishing arm.

Pat calls Ed her champion. She says he taught her everything she knows about the marketing business. He was in business for a total of 57 years and she worked by his side until he retired in 1990 after his business was sold.

I asked Pat to tell me a war story about gender discrimination, and she shared one about one of their clients, a large organization. "I was in charge of the account," she says, "doing the lion's share of the work. Ed and I attended the meetings together, but he did all the talking. I would literally hand him the reports seconds before we got on the elevator. At the client's offices, the men would make sexist comments right in front of me. In the rare instances when I attended a meeting without Ed and made recommendations, they'd ask, 'Don't you have to ask Ed about this first?' I'd say, 'No, usually Ed comes back to the office and asks *me.*'"

Another time, Pat was invited to an important meeting with a group of men from the client's office. "Their leader asked me what I'd like to drink, specifically, what cocktail I liked to drink," she says. "I said I liked gin and tonic, and the waiter brought me *four* of them in tall water glasses. I must have looked worried, because the client said, 'Don't worry. I'll help you down those.' The men drank several tall glasses of alcohol." That was a hot, summer day, and Pat cried all the way home, barely able to see the road through her tears. To her, this lunch meeting was a disaster.

"But the next day, when I went into the office," she says, "Ed was waiting for me. He had just spoken with the client. I crumbled into hysterics. 'I'm so sorry,' I said. 'We were doing so well with this account.' But Ed chuckled. 'You misunderstand,' he said. 'From now on, they want you at *all* of the meetings.'"

A year later, the first woman in the agency's history became a department head in charge of human resources. She and Pat were the only two women at staff meetings and important functions. "But we never sat together," Pat recalls. "We wanted to show these men that we were equals, that we earned our positions on merit and didn't need to sit together like cowering women."

Gauge grew rapidly after Pat joined the company, and she recognized early on that she wasn't great at managing people. "Marilyn Stevens, who was my right hand person at Forester & Company, pointed out something that I hadn't realized about myself," Pat says. "I always told new hires to take his or her time, learn the business, and to not work as hard as I did because I didn't expect anyone else to work as hard as I did. Marilyn told me to stop saying that to people, because in fact, I *did* expect people to work as hard as I did."

Pat couldn't understand that everyone wasn't ready to show up early every day with smiles on their faces ready to rock in the highly stressful environment.

"Gauge was an aggressive workplace," Pat says. "We had an office on the fifth floor at 12th and Market Streets in Wilmington, Del. We had account executives, graphic designers, and lots of clients and complete chaos every single day. I kept two suits in my office so I'd always be ready for anything. I loved it."

But, wait! She had a family, didn't she? Young boys? A husband?

"I honestly don't know how we did it," Pat says, "but when my kids got involved with something, I never missed a thing. I do remember sometimes getting up at 4 a.m. so I could go to the office and work for a few hours, but really, my family always came first. People would tell me that I couldn't do everything, and I'd say, 'Watch me.' There was sacrifice, sure. I always tell people to go where the business takes you, but be sure it enriches your life, not takes you away from what truly matters. Don't worry so much about the money. If you are in business solely to make money, you will fail. Provide a good product and service, and the money will take care of itself. I was determined to have a good, full life, to be passionate, confident and tenacious. My father taught me that."

After Ed's retirement, Pat started Forester Communications and continued to support a full client roster until 2006, when her husband became ill. "I sold the business and did any freelance job I could from home," she says. "The clients I have today are the ones who stayed with me. My son, Terry, was in Iraq for his first tour. He was gone for two years and we heard from him only three times. My husband had to be watched 24 hours a day."

Once again, as we talked, Pat drifted again, deep in thought and left seemingly with just her memories. But this time, she spoke up. "My five boys: they were it for us," she says. "They are the wonderful husbands and fathers they are today because we raised them that way."

Many attended Jerry's funeral, since his family was large and he had countless friends. But four days after his service, Pat put on her game face and attended a chamber of commerce event she'd been planning for a year.

"I had no choice but to go," she says. "Two days later, I was driving on a beautiful day and I broke down, just started sobbing. I asked everyone, even my boys, to just leave me alone for a while so that I could feel the feelings. I slept a lot and sat alone in my jammies feeling sorry for myself. During Jerry's illness, we went through our entire life's savings, but he got very good care. You just have to do what you have to do. It was very difficult to watch all that money we'd worked so hard for go away. But then, after a few days, I remembered who I was. I remembered that I'm a hard worker, and that I can always make money. And because I'm a worker, I had never intended to retire in the first place. I've always had a five-year plan. I realized that despite everything, I was going to be all right."

A year later, on a Friday morning, Pat's vision blurred so badly she couldn't see. She called 911, and the operator asked her to stay on the phone until the emergency crew arrived.

"The next thing I remember is waking up in the hospital with my boys around me," she says. "I had had a massive stroke and the doctors had paralyzed my body to stave off its effects and save my life. I was so unstable that they couldn't do an MRI until the following Tuesday morning. I was in the hospital for 10 days, and then recuperated at my son Bob's home in New Jersey. I could not see well or speak for months."

But she recovered. In 2010, Pat and her mother bought a home in a 55-plus community in Delaware. When Pat took her mother to social functions, she introduced her as the original Wonder Woman.

"You know, I was a Wonder Woman, way ahead of my time in the 1960s, and it wasn't my intention," Pat says. "I think it's because of my love for what I feel I was born to do. I'm a born marketer. I'll talk to anybody. I love to seek out new people and try to make them clients."

Pat's Final Thoughts

"It was the dark ages for women when I came up through the ranks. There were only a few women in Delaware running businesses. It was definitely a man's world. I had a male client once say to me, 'Pat, this isn't personal, this is business.' It made me start watching the women around me. They verbalize their feelings. Well, nobody cares. This isn't about you! It's business. My biggest piece of advice is: If you know what you're doing, and it's the right thing to do, have confidence and keep pushing until it gets done. Keep going. Try not to get discouraged. You're going to be all right. Building a business takes a lot of determination, passion and the desire to do good work. I have never seen anyone build a successful business on money alone."

Jane Golden

Jane Golden

"It never occurred to me that being female could in any way impede me. I never thought that being a woman meant that I couldn't do certain things."

Biography

Jane Golden is the founder and executive director of the City of Philadelphia Mural Arts Program (Mural Arts). Under the driving force of her direction, Mural Arts has created more than 3,800 works of public art through innovative collaborations with community-based organizations, city agencies, nonprofit organizations, schools, the private sector and philanthropists.

Through these partnerships, she has developed creative and rigorous programs in youth art education, restorative justice and behavioral health that have made it possible for thousands to experience and witness the power of art. She has also overseen a series of increasingly complex, ambitious and award-winning public art projects, and is currently sought after nationally and internationally as an expert on urban transformation through art.

Jane has received numerous awards for her work, including the Philadelphia Award, the Visionary Woman Award from Moore College of Art, the 2012 Governor's Award for Innovation in the Arts, an Eisenhower Exchange Fellowship Award, and Philadelphia Magazine's Trailblazer Award.

She has also co-authored two books about the murals in Philadelphia and co-edited a third, "Mural Arts @ 30" (Temple University Press, 2014), published on the occasion of Mural Arts' 30th anniversary.

Jane holds an MFA from the Mason Gross School of the Arts at Rutgers University, and degrees in Fine Arts and Political Science from Stanford University. Also, she has received honorary doctorates from Swarthmore College, Philadelphia's University of the Arts, Widener University, Arcadia University, LaSalle College, Haverford College, Rosemont College and Villanova University.

Jane's Story

Jane Golden has overcome a personal obstacle in her life that forced her, while a young woman, to look death in the face. Something happens to you when you survive threats to your very existence. In Jane's case, I think it gave her super powers.

Jane is a magnetic and inspiring speaker, to say the least. She is electricity in human form, exuding energy and confidence. It's her passion for her job, combined with the life energy she acquired when she grabbed onto her new lease on life with fanatical vigor, that made her determined to make every day count—not only for herself but for others as well—using art as her healing instrument and catalyst for positive change.

She was born to Gloria and Sanford Golden in Minneapolis, Minn. Her brother Jonathan, whom Jane describes as "one of my favorite people," was born four-and-a-half years later. When she was five, the family moved to the New Jersey shore. Jane grew up in Margate.

Jane adores her parents and says she had a healthy childhood. "Our house was no more than 100 feet from the ocean, so we were a dedicated beach family," she says. "We surfed, sailed, had kayaks and used skimboards. I loved growing up at the shore."

Jane's mother, Gloria, was a gifted watercolor artist. "When I was little, I would watch her paint. I think my love of art came from her. She encouraged me to take watercolor classes, and sometimes she'd paint with me. She was an unusual person, incredibly smart, honest and direct. She would have been a great lawyer."

Sanford was a businessman who owned a collection of stores called the China Outlet Gourmet Garage. He started out in the oil and gasoline business with Gloria's father, but left to pursue his dream of going into retail.

"He started teeny, and then it grew because he was very creative," says Jane. "He believed that people could get great things for very low prices, so his retail philosophy was popular. My mom did the buying for the stores because she had such an artistic eye, and she was uncanny. She had an instinct for knowing what people would buy. She had great taste and it showed in the way she decorated our home, the way she dressed—everything."

Both of Jane's parents were lovers of the arts, and she remembers them taking her and her brother to art galleries and museums. They often went up to New York City. Her parents, especially her father, were in love with the art created during the Works Progress Administration, which was renamed in 1930 as the Work Projects Administration (WPA). One of its programs, the Federal Project Number One, employed musicians, artists, writers, actors and directors.

"Because they received support from the Federal government, some extraordinary art was produced during that period," says Jane.

When she was little, Jane pored over art books for hours, attracted to paintings by muralists Thomas Hart Benton, Ben Shahn and Grant Wood.

"They were my heroes, so I think of myself as having grown up with a mural-friendly family," says Jane.

Jane says her father instilled in her the feeling that she had to work very hard, that there were no shortcuts, and that it was important always to be humble, gracious and grateful.

"I was an annoying overachiever," Jane says. "I took piano for nine years. I was an excellent student. I brought roses to teachers. I stayed after school and did the bulletin boards. I wanted to do well, and I was highly competitive. I was just wired that way."

Jane's parents encouraged their daughter to be independent, and they assured her that she could be anything she wanted in life. "It never occurred to me that being female could in any way impede me," she says. "I never thought that being a woman meant that I couldn't do certain things. Still, I'm sometimes annoyed when people say, 'Jane's a pest.' What they'd say about a man is, 'Oh, that man is so tenacious.' Otherwise, seeing women as having a disadvantage has never factored into my world view."

Jane decided she wanted to be a detective, so she organized a spy club. Because she was the founder, she named herself 007. She chose the names for everyone else, too, including her little brother's, who she teased by naming him 00-minus-35. He wasn't so happy about that.

"He's 6-foot-five now, and an important attorney who's quite brilliant," Jane laughs. "I stopped picking on him a long time ago!"

When she was in the seventh grade, Jane had a teacher who encouraged her love of reading. "I remember the world of literature opening up for me," she says. "My dad brought home books every week, American novels that were relatively dense and esoteric, like "An American Tragedy," by Theodore Dreiser. I challenged myself to read those books. It was a wonderful experience."

Another great teacher, Miriam Jameson, further instilled in Jane her already simmering love of arts and culture. "She had a beautiful home in Longport," Jane recalls. "You could see the ocean, and her studio was filled with seashells. She was in the American Watercolor Society, so she was quite a brilliant watercolor painter. She'd lost her child to polio, and so treated me like a daughter. We'd listen to classical music, and paint. She read me stories about famous artists like Monet and Van Gogh. I went every week."

In high school, on Saturdays, Jane and her best friend took the bus to Philadelphia to take classes at the Museum of Art.

"After my junior year, I had the good fortune to go with a group of students to Florence, Italy for the summer," she says. "As I look back at those times, I realize that I was quite introverted and lived in the world of my imagination. I invented worlds."

Upon high school graduation, Jane went to Mount Holyoke College in Massachusetts, majoring in art and political science. During the first winter break, however, someone suggested she attend Stanford.

"My cousin, Michael Goldberg, was a well-known abstract painter," she says. "I was looking for internships, so he recommended a painter for whom I swept floors and made canvases. It was pretty mundane, but I met some extraordinary people. This painter suggested I transfer to Stanford, because they were looking for serious students. I applied and got in. My teachers were some of the top California painters, so those next three years were a big treat."

After graduating, Jane followed friends to Los Angeles, where she got a job at a daycare center. It was chaotic and paid only minimum wage, so she didn't enjoy it.

"I wasn't a very good waitress, either," says Jane. "I wasn't happy at any of my jobs, and I felt isolated painting alone in my studio. I'd tried lots of things—yoga, tutoring, a drawing class—but nothing felt right. Then, I read an article about a mural program in Los Angeles."

Jane called the city to ask about filling out a grant application to become a part of the program. They told her she was ineligible because she'd missed the deadline. Jane Golden doesn't hear the word *no*.

"I said, 'What would I have had to do to apply for the grant?' They told me I needed to find a wall, hire people from the neighborhood, and create a design about a community issue. I said, 'okay, thanks.' I went out and researched the community. I found a place at the end of a street where there had once been an amusement park. It had been torn down, and the locals were unhappy about it. It reminded me of how Atlantic City used to be, so I did a design based on that."

Jane walked around the neighborhood and introduced herself to people. She found a team who said they'd paint the mural with her if she could get the paint.

"Then, I knocked on the door of a building that had a large, blank wall," she continues. "I asked the man if I could paint a mural on his wall, and he said, 'Sure.' It was very strange. He'd never seen my work. He simply agreed."

Jane called the city again and told them she'd done everything they'd required. She asked them to reconsider letting her apply for the grant. Again, they said no.

"So, I drove downtown and dropped off my application," she says. "And then, I called them every day for three months. I was only 22, but I'd honed my skills. One day, they called me. 'Is this Jane Golden?' the voice asked. I said yes. 'We hope never to hear from you again, but you have the grant.' I was thrilled. That grant changed my life."

Interestingly, Jane had never painted a mural before. She called the city of Chicago, which had a mural program, and was sent a booklet of instructions. She still has it. Its pages are dog-eared and underlined.

Jane says the murals in Venice and other areas were fantastic. "There was one that was probably seven stories tall, with a picture of Los Angeles after an earthquake. It was called, 'The Freeway Disaster.' There was another called, 'L.A. in the Snow,' which was also beautiful."

She went back to the amusement park area and reintroduced herself to the neighbors. They all agreed to work with her, and together they painted the first large mural in Santa Monica. Jane Fonda, who lived down the street, did the dedication.

"People told me I should get a celebrity to dedicate the mural," says Jane (Golden). I said, 'I'm a 22-year-old from New Jersey. I don't know anyone famous!' But it was a great idea, so, covered with paint, I walked down the street and knocked on her door. She answered. I asked if she'd please cut the ribbon."

Jane Fonda said, "Oh, I've seen you working. I love to see women working that way. I've seen you carrying paint and moving the scaffolding. Is there anything else I can do to help you?"

Jane Golden said, "Yes! Would you bring all of your friends?"

It was a coup.

After painting several more murals, Jane and her friends created the Public Arts Foundation, where they worked with kids on probation.

"That's around the time I got sick," says Jane. "I was tired all of the time, had fevers and a rash over my cheeks and nose."

Her diagnosis: two kinds of lupus—discoid and systemic. Lupus is an autoimmune disease in which the body creates autoantibodies that attack and destroy healthy tissue.

"The discoid lupus is somewhat disfiguring, so I had scarring on my face," she says. "And it's painful. I was hospitalized for it."

Jane left Los Angeles and moved in with her parents so she could receive treatment at Hahnemann Hospital. "Being diagnosed with a serious illness changes your perspective," says Jane. "It changes your sense of time and creates a greater sense of urgency. I became more empathetic and saw myself for the first time as an outsider, not somebody who was destined to live to be 100 with a charmed life."

She got a job at the Anti-Graffiti Network in Philadelphia and started meeting kids who had not grown up with the same privileges that she'd known growing up. "It startled me to realize that I identified with them in some way," she says. "They felt like outsiders, and so did I. I also felt lucky and grateful and felt that those of us who have privilege need to figure out what to do with it. It was an epiphany that was both reassuring and life affirming."

Something new was born in Jane when she started working with kids who were former graffiti writers. She saw them as artists who had never had the opportunity to express their talent. They were creating in neighborhoods destroyed by crime, violence and poverty. "We gave them the opportunity to create art as a city service, art that became a beacon and catalyst. It was extraordinary, and over time, I forgot my lupus," Jane says. "I knew I'd probably be sick on and off, so I decided to hope for the best, take good care of myself, and just concentrate on trying to make Philadelphia a really great city filled with art."

Since 1984, the Mural Arts Program has created 3,800 murals. "I think Anti-Graffiti was a great training ground, because I had to overcome so many obstacles all the time," says Jane. "Essentially, it was a cleanup program. We were working in neighborhoods where people were struggling, and the only other visible city workers were police officers. There were always dramas. Our kids sometimes got involved in drugs or shootings. We'd go up two steps, then down 10 steps. I think I learned to deal with a lot of complexity early on."

Jane met her husband, Anthony, through a mutual friend who thought the two might get along. They met, but didn't go out until a year later.

"For his day job, he does communications for the American Friends Service Committee, a Quaker service organization," Jane says. "But really, he's a documentary filmmaker. He and his colleagues did a film about our mural work in prisons. It's called, 'Concrete, Steel & Paint.' It's won a number of awards."

Jane describes herself as someone who is very results oriented. "I feel like if we're going to do this work, we have to do it really well, which means that there's some impact, that something is changing, that we're moving the needle. It gives me great pleasure to know that we have figured out a way to use art in a very practical way. Our program is both aspirational and highly pragmatic, and I love that."

Jane is a very busy person. She teaches at the University of Pennsylvania and at Moore College of Art, which she enjoys.

"We're talking about creating a Mural Arts University, which would work with cities all over the world, which is exciting," she says, "and I just got back from Cuba. We're going to do a project there. There are many options going forward. Eventually, I can see myself doing consulting work."

I have no doubt that Jane will continue to do interesting work and, like her mother used to say, "walking where angels fear to tread."

Jane's Final Thoughts

I am someone who is blessed because I can wake up every day to do work that I love. I feel like my work has a place in this world, which is unusual.

My parents instilled in me a deep sense of the importance of giving back, but also, they wanted me to follow my bliss. Here's an example. When Anti-Graffiti closed down, I applied to law school, and my brother tried to talk me out of it. He thought I should run an art program for the city. "But there isn't one," I argued. "Then, go start one," he said. So, I went to Ed Rendell, who created the Mural Arts Program, and he offered me the director position.

I was torn. My father said to me, "If you really want to run an art program for the city, then have the courage not to go to law school." I thought that was brave of him because I know he would have rather had me do something that offered more security.

So I followed my heart, and my parents were proud.

Guillermina González

Guillermina González

"Each night, before I go to sleep, I pray to have the capacity of discernment and wisdom. That's all I want to have."

Biography

Dr. Guillermina González is the executive director of the Delaware Arts Alliance, a highly active arts advocacy group in the state. Previously, she served as executive director of the advocacy organization, Voices Without Borders. She is a multicultural professional with experience in the United States, Mexico and Europe, and has enjoyed a successful career as an executive in the corporate and nonprofit sectors.

Guillermina is actively involved in the community and serves as the chair of the Americans for the Arts' State Arts Action Network as well as Delaware's NPR WDDE Community Advisory Board. She has served on the Delaware State Arts Council, and on the boards of Delaware College of Art and Design, Metropolitan Wilmington Urban League, Latin American Community Center, and the AARP Executive Council.

An active media commentator, Guillermina has been featured in print media in The News Journal, Delaware Today magazine, Signature Brandywine, Delaware's El Tiempo Hispano, and Voz Latina magazine. She is a radio host for a program called "Delaware State of the Arts" (1450 WILM News Radio/1410 WDOV), and "Latinisimo" (91.3 WVUD), the University of Delaware's only Spanish-speaking program, on which she had the privilege of interviewing Mario Vargas Llosa, the 2010 Nobel Prize winner. She also co-hosted "The Latin Beat" (1150 WDEL) for eight years.

Guillermina earned an MBA from Universidad Iberoamericana in Mexico City, where she later taught marketing and business administration. She holds a Certificate in Leadership and Public Management and a master's in Liberal Studies from the University of Delaware, and obtained her Doctorate in Business Administration (DBA) at Wilmington University in January of 2014.

Guillermina's Story

Dear reader, I wish you had been with me when Guillermina González and I talked. You need to see her in action—not just read about her. I wanted you sitting in the chair beside me; to hear her voice, tone, inflections, and the way she pronounces words with her cultivated Spanish accent. I wanted you to be able to see her face, so alive with expression and humor. Guillermina's personality and delivery are feasts for the senses, a portrait of exuberance and youth. Can words even suffice? Certainly not, but I will try.

Guillermina and I first met at an event where she was part of a panel discussion with other distinguished women in the arts. Representing the Delaware Arts Alliance, the unifying voice for the arts throughout the state for which she is executive director, Guillermina spoke with authority and passion of the many issues and challenges facing the arts. It's too bad fist pumps aren't appropriate in polite gatherings!

Named after her mother, Guillermina López de González, Guillermina was born in Mexico City, the oldest of four children. She says she grew up in an "intellectual household," and describes her childhood as typical and happy. Her mother, also a Mexico City native, was a chemist by profession who quit working once she married, as was the custom. Guillermina says she was a wonderful mother.

"She always empowered me," Guillermina says. "She encouraged me to try new things, and provided a warm, nurturing environment. I remember her reading to us and creating piñatas from scratch. We were never wealthy, but she managed money so well that we missed out on nothing. We were all very well educated. She made magic with what little we had."

Guillermina says she learned early from her mother the importance of being a good role model, and that as the oldest, it was her duty to set an example for her siblings. "She taught me how to handle myself well," says Guillermina. "She'd say, 'Your siblings are watching you.' I always sensed the need to do everything right. I don't recommend it—it's a heavy burden for a child."

Her father, Dr. Héctor González, who passed away two years ago at 81, was from Tamaulipas, a Mexican state that borders Texas. "He was a neurosurgeon by profession, and was very intelligent," Guillermina says. "When I picture him in my mind, he is reading something. He had difficulties relating to us, in the sense that raising a family was an intellectual exercise for him. He was a nice guy with a good sense of humor, but not necessarily the nurturing type. My mother and her family balanced it all out. They were loud, affectionate huggers."

Guillermina says that touching is an important part of the Latin American culture. The notion of personal space is quite different than in North America, where we tend to feel uncomfortable when someone violates it.

"The space around us in Latin America is much less," explains Guillermina. "We give more of ourselves more quickly. It's one of the first, major cultural differences I noticed when I came to the U.S."

Guillermina was an intelligent and inquisitive child. She read everything she could get her hands on, and everything interested her, so much so that she couldn't decide what she wanted to be when she grew up.

"I felt torn in so many different directions," she says. "I explored being a lawyer, an economist, a doctor, a chemist—you name it. My mother encouraged it, and made me feel successful in everything I tried."

A career in the arts hadn't occurred to her, although a love for the arts is in her DNA—an important part of her family's lives. "Our weekends were filled with trips to the museum or symphony," says Guillermina. "Our parents instilled in us a passion for the arts. We were always listening to classical music or music in general. We didn't always have money for tickets, but my mother usually found a free concert or event."

Guillermina never felt she was treated differently because she was female. Rather, her parents continually reinforced the idea that she could do whatever she wanted in life. Her father believed that women and men were intellectual equals.

"There was one rare time when my mother suggested to my sisters and me that we ought to serve our brother," Guillermina says, with a laugh. "And we said, 'No way! Doesn't he have hands?' My mother never pressured me to marry early, either. Most young women got married early. I told my mother that I would never marry unless I found the right match, and I remember her telling me that that was a good decision. I felt empowered by this."

While her mother was fairly liberal, allowing her oldest daughter the freedom to pursue her unique interests, she also established strong boundaries that the siblings knew not to cross. Then again, the parental authority was not so strict. After all, Guillermina was an inquisitive teenager.

"I just wanted to excel in everything I did," says Guillermina. "I was always intellectually stimulated: reading and learning. I loved history. I was good at numbers, but they weren't my cup of tea. When it came time to decide what to study at a prestigious Mexican university, I chose chemical engineering. My mom was really excited about that, because she's a chemist. I realized soon after I started that chemical engineering wasn't my cup of tea either. But my mother was very understanding and gave me the freedom to change my major."

Eighteen-year-old Guillermina agonized over where to focus her studies. People had always told her she was good at everything, and if that was so, and because she loved so many different things, how could she possibly focus on just one thing?

"And then I found the solution," she says. "I chose business administration, because it had a little bit of everything. I loved it so much that I went on to earn my doctorate in it, and I even teach it at Wilmington University."

Guillermina found employment with a consulting firm before completing her bachelor's degree, and later worked in marketing and sales for large corporations including Mars and ExxonMobil among others. Her intention was to become a marketing guru for the company, but life had other plans.

"I felt the need for bigger challenges in the company, so I told my boss that I needed a change," she says. "Suddenly, I found myself talking with the director of the North American operations (Canada, U.S. and Mexico). She invited me to come to the U.S. on an expatriate assignment. I was single, so I went for it!"

It was a fateful decision, and within the space of a year, her entire life changed.

Her plans, as well as the expectations of her management, had been to work in the Fairfax, VA area for three years, then return to

Mexico to take on another assignment elsewhere. The ExxonMobil merger took a different shape and the company needed her back in Mexico earlier than anticipated. That triggered a marriage proposal that left her outside ExxonMobil.

"I went from living in Mexico to living in the U.S.," says Guillermina. "I went from being single to being married. I had an excellent job with a brilliant future, and then here I was, unemployed.

"Talk about challenges!" she adds. "Here I was in a strange country, thinking, 'What have I done?' Except for my fiancé, I knew no one and had no family nearby.

Guillermina met her husband, Charles, on an airplane in 2001, shortly after she arrived in the U.S. She'd been visiting West Virginia as part of her duties as the National Accounts representative for the Mid-Atlantic region. Charles was a DuPont executive working at its Parkersburg plant. She boarded a plane in Parkersburg to fly to the Washington, D.C. area.

"It was a tiny, commuter plane," she says. "Have you ever been on one of those? I was terrified, and I began talking to the nearest person I could find, who was the man sitting next to me. It was Charles."

He was everything she was looking for in a partner, the Yin to her Yang. "Charles is an extremely intelligent guy, gifted even," says Guillermina. "He has a Ph.D. in chemical engineering from CalTech. I didn't know how famous CalTech was until my sister, an engineer herself, told me. I liked that he had a Ph.D., because it showed me he was a man who was willing to make an effort," she says, with a laugh, adding that while Charles has a great sense of humor, the two are polar opposites.

"He's a numbers guy, very detail oriented, and I'm not," she says. "I'm very talkative and outgoing, and he's an introvert. But we have such fun, and he enjoys himself immensely when we're together and with other people."

Charles helped his wife improve her English speaking skills and adjust to American culture. "Charles (not his real name; his real name in Spanish is Carlos) was born in Argentina," she says. "He came to the U.S. with the family when he was one, because his father got a scholarship. He thinks in English, and considers himself an American with Argentine heritage."

I asked her what it was like adjusting to life in a new country and a new language? Was there any discrimination, gender or otherwise?

"Not gender discrimination," Guillermina says. "I was raised in an empowering household that taught me how to be assertive. But there was some racial discrimination after arriving to the U.S. I remember one woman making a comment about my English. I called her out on it, explaining it was racist, and she apologized. You know, I don't think with an accent, actually."

While at Exxon in Mexico, Guillermina was often the only woman at meetings. "It gave me a competitive advantage, actually," she says. "They wanted a skilled professional who happened to be a woman and non-engineer on the all-male executive team for the sake of diversity."

Guillermina says she had a wonderful mentor at Exxon, a man who has remained a friend. I thought this was interesting: More than half of the women I've interviewed for "Pearls" have reported having had male mentors who have helped advance their careers. Guillermina has an explanation for this.

"There are not enough women in executive-level positions," she says. "There was an article in The Wall Street Journal a few years ago saying that the fact that there are still very few women in the upper echelons of management is a sign that gender bias still exists and must be acknowledged. Until women break this barrier, there will be fewer women mentors. In contrast, there have been more women presidents in Latin America than there have been in the U.S.

"Let me give you some examples," she adds. "There is Dilma Rouseff in Brazil right now; Christina Fernandez de Kirchner in Argentina (who recently stepped down); and Michelle Bachelet in Chile. You'd expect more women to be in power in the U.S., but it's just the opposite. It's interesting, is it not?"

It certainly is. Yet, Guillermina doesn't consider herself to be a leader, but rather a dot connector, someone who favors consensus whenever possible. Still, she's not afraid to make decisions.

"I typically gather information and input from people of all sorts, and then make a decision when I've thoroughly assessed the situation," she says. "I think, however, that the concept of leadership, particularly in this country, is fading. People tend to equate leadership to spotlight seekers and celebrity types. My definition of leadership is the opposite. You don't have to show off to be a leader. If you claim yourself to be a leader, that's the minute you're not. To be a leader, you don't have to claim anything. You don't have to demonstrate what is evident.

"You command conviction, and you command a message that people believe in," she continues. "Therefore, as a consequence, you rise to that position, but not because you were seeking it. It's not an objective—it just happens."

One of the biggest influences on Guillermina's view of leadership and power was her maternal grandfather, an "accidental" politician.

"I come from a political family," she explains. "My grandfather said that politics was all about serving people. That's all he said. It was a big part of the conversation when we all got together— birthdays, breakfast and gatherings. Frequently, presidents and elected officials sat beside indigenous people and everyone was served equally. We were told to treat everyone with profound respect regardless of their origin, particularly those people, because they were *his* people."

Guillermina has lived these principles, but also enjoys life. For fun, she and Charles go to the movies, particularly Theater N at Nemours in downtown Wilmington, where they can also enjoy a glass of wine.

"I like to keep myself occupied," she says. "These days, teaching classes besides my full time position as executive director keeps me really busy. I don't have a 9-to 5-type of occupation, but I do have to do whatever is needed, sometimes on weekends. I think I'm going to be here doing what I'm doing as long as it's fun and I don't become the organization. I will probably step down at the top of my game, when I see that the organization is strong enough for a succession plan. That's something that I talk to my board about. I'm not going to be here forever. And I want the organization to be stronger than it was when I first arrived."

Always exploring, Guillermina has thought about the possibility of teaching more, but she's not convinced herself yet.

"As long as I can find a place where I can continue being the dot connector, I might entertain the idea of switching gears," she says. "I learned from my life-changing experience in 2001 that I have to remain open to whatever might come along. Something out there is going to come along. I have the sense that this is not my final destination, that there is something else I still need to do. Good times are about to come. What that is going to be, I don't know. But I'm not worried about it.

"While growing up, I was taught empowerment," she adds. "And so I tell you, just be who you are, and have great pride. Carry yourself with clear values, keep yourself clean, intellectually and emotionally speaking. If you are able to be yourself, regardless of where you are, you will always sleep well. That's when you know you are doing good things. Each night, before I sleep, I pray to have the capacity of discernment and wisdom. That's all I want to have."

Guillermina's Final Thoughts

In 2001, my world fell apart, and I had to reinvent myself. I felt naked, intellectually speaking. My definition of myself was very much related to how successful I was in corporate America, and how recognized I would become at a great company like ExxonMobil. They wouldn't have invested in me if they hadn't seen that I had what it took. Leaving that behind was frightening, to say the least.

DuPont helped me with career transitioning, and there was an expert who provided an assessment that was the most complete assessment I have ever taken. The Highlands Battery Test measures you in nine dimensions. I learned things about myself that I didn't know, and it pointed me in a good direction. It made me reflect on my values, the kind of environment I liked, and how I learn. These characteristics, according to the expert, change every 10 years. So the individual you were 10 years ago is not the individual you are right now, and not the individual you will be in the next 10 years. People evolve. I like that idea.

Sarah Ives Gore & Molly

66

Sarah Ives Gore

"Keep the faith. Remember that you are a good person and God is looking out for you."

Biography

Sally Gore retired in 2005 as the global leader of the W. L. Gore & Associates, Inc. human resources team. When she joined Gore 25 years earlier, Gore had no human resources function. Hired to help coordinate interviewing and hiring, Sally grew her team of one into a global HR organization of more than 100 people.

Before joining Gore, Sally taught elementary school and worked as a counselor. Support of education is a theme that runs through her personal and professional life. She was instrumental in the startup of the Option Program, a program for disruptive high school adolescents in New Castle County, Delaware. Sally and her family also created the I Have a Dream Foundation of Delaware.

A graduate of the College of William & Mary with a bachelor's in English, Sally remains active at her alma mater, and has supported the construction of both a childcare center and an interdisciplinary science center on campus. She also holds a master's in counseling from the University of Delaware, where she and her husband provided the financial support for the construction of Gore Hall. She is currently on the Board of the College of Education and Human Development there.

Long committed to service to Delaware and its communities, Sally served on the Delaware Health Care Commission from 1990 to 1994, and as its chairperson from 1993 to 1994. She currently serves on the boards of Girl Scouts of Chesapeake Bay, Christiana Care Health System, Kind to Kids (advocates to children in foster care), Vision to Learn (helping underprivileged children obtain their glasses), Serviam Girls Academy (a tuition-free, independent middle school for young women from low-income families). Sally also chairs the Middle Run Philanthropic Foundation.

Sally's Story

It is difficult to get Sally Gore to talk about herself. It's not because she's shy, reticent or has nothing to say. In fact, she's extremely warm and outgoing, with many impressive things she *could* say about herself.

To illustrate her modesty, we were more than an hour into our conversation before she mentioned that her son, Chris Coons, was a United States senator, and even then, I had to pry it out of her. I already knew that, of course, but she wasn't bringing it up. That fascinated me.

Sally would much rather talk about issues beyond herself that feed souls and fuel compassion, like the magic of a Girl Scout experience, or how so many children don't succeed in school because their family can't afford eyeglasses—a problem she decided to address. Originally a teacher by training and then a human resources executive by accident, Sally envisions possibilities, sees past limitations, develops practical solutions, and then does the work to make things happen.

Sarah Louise "Sally" Ives was born New York City. Her parents, Andrew McCormack Ives and Carolyn Countryman Ives, moved often because of Andrew's job. Thus, Sally's older sister, Peg (Margaret), was born in Los Angeles and her younger brother, Drew (Andrew, Jr.), in Chicago.

"My dad was a mechanical engineer for Swift & Company, a meat packing company," says Sally. "He was the sort of engineer who could fix anything, so I assumed all engineers could fix anything. I later discovered that there were two kinds of engineers: the ones who fix things, and the conceptual ones. At Swift, Sally's father was in charge of building new facilities—a slaughterhouse, a leather factory, an ice cream plant—all around the country.

"When I was a small child, I remember being in California and starting kindergarten," Sally says. "Then we moved to Seattle, where I started first grade. I finished first grade in Chicago, and I finished second grade in Louisiana. Peg and I were best friends, because we were constants in each other's lives. But I didn't find having to make new friends difficult. I'm an extrovert, and can pretty much talk to anybody."

Sally recalls having felt like an outsider in her family, because her personality was very different from everyone else's.

"Are you familiar with the Myers Briggs personality tests? My brother and I are ENFPs (Extroverted, Intuitive, Feeling, Perceiving) who become teachers, or preachers, or people who sell things," she says. "My mother, sister and father are very different from me in the ways their minds work. It made for an interesting family dynamic, and sometimes I felt I was a stubborn child because I didn't fit into the mainstream point of view."

She was a good student who skipped second grade and graduated from high school when she was barely 17. "For two summers while I was in college, my folks lived in Marblehead, Massachusetts. I ran the waterfront for the YMCA day camp," Sally explains. "It's a job with a lot of responsibility. You always have to come home with the same number of children you left with. We took a ferry every morning to a big piece of rock in the harbor called Children's Island, which was loaded with seagulls, and one single, small building where we'd eat lunch, make crafts, and afterwards, do some swimming. It was a wonderful adventure."

Sally was a long-time, passionate Girl Scout and continues her commitment and advocacy as co-chair of its $6.8 million capital campaign to build a new facility.

"The first time I got to go to Girl Scout camp, I was about ten," she says. "My mother said I had to learn to braid my own hair before I could go. Camp, to me, was the most amazing, wonderful adventure in the world. In my high school years, I became a senior counselor at a Girl Scout camp in far northern Wisconsin. I learned so many skills! In today's world, Girl Scouts are doing many different things besides camping, and I've always thought of them as positive role models for young women."

Sally never gave much thought to what she'd be when she grew up. Her mother was a teacher, so she figured she'd be a teacher, too. There were fewer career options for women in the 1950s.

"When I was a freshman at The College of William & Mary in Virginia, I wanted to major in chemistry," she says, "and my mother said, 'Honey, girls don't do that.' I argued with her. After all, I said, there was one girl in my sorority who was majoring in chemistry. But she insisted that I major in either English or French, so I majored in

English. I always did what was expected of me—it's how my family worked."

Her college years were transformative, and Sally loved her time there.

"I arrived at school with the idea that I was supposed to do everything," Sally says. "I was supposed to get really good grades, run for office, work for the school newspaper *and* date lots of boys. So, I was on the judicial council and joined a sorority, Kappa Kappa Gamma. Sororities provide great opportunities for leadership, make you feel included, and encourage you to do your best. College was a wonderful four years for me. I loved it."

After graduation, Sally and a friend went to Greenwich, Connecticut, to teach third grade in two separate elementary schools.

"We bought a second-hand car together, and I'd drop her off in the morning and then drive to my school," Sally says. "We lived in a big, old house with six young women and had a fabulous time. We had parties every weekend; women brought food and men brought the booze. It's how I met Ken, my first husband. He lived in a house in Darien with six young men. In the middle of my second year in Connecticut, we got married and moved into an apartment in Stamford."

A couple of years later, Sally got pregnant. In those days, teachers were expected to leave their jobs within three months.

"They didn't want the children to know their teachers were pregnant," Sally explains. "I didn't want to leave my kids—I loved them as if they were mine—so I didn't tell my principal I was pregnant and taught until the end of my pregnancy."

Sally and Ken bought a house and had two more children, Chris and Steve. Two years after Steve was born, Ken's job changed and the family moved to Timonium, Maryland, a town outside Baltimore. Two years later, they moved to Hockessin, Delaware.

"We built a house in a development called Walnut Hill, which was so close to the kids' school that all they had to do every morning was walk across the backyard," says Sally. "Those were wonderful years, raising the kids and living our busy, day-to-day lives."

In 1974, Sally's life took an unexpected turn after her husband purchased a cabinet manufacturing company in Baltimore.

"It was terrible timing," she says. "There was an oil crisis that year and people were waiting in lines for an hour or more just to buy gas. The economy, too, was in trouble, and banks were calling in loans. They called in my husband's loan on his new company, and it bankrupted the company. Ken left us and went to Rhode Island to work at a friend's company, and eventually we divorced."

Meanwhile, Sally had gone back to school to earn her graduate degree and was working as a teacher.

"The previous year, while Steve was in kindergarten, I taught sixth grade and was appalled to realize the schools had turned into zoos," Sally says. "It was as if all the kids had suddenly lost their minds, as well as their respect for the teachers. I decided I wanted to get another degree and become a clinical psychologist."

She started at the University of Delaware, but after one semester, Ken's company went bankrupt and she realized she didn't have enough money to continue. "Thankfully, the University of Delaware agreed to waive the tuition if I would work 20 hours a week counseling seniors," she says.

Sally worked from 8 a.m. to noon, five days a week; gave piano lessons to 30 students from 3 to 6 p.m., and attended class most nights from 7 to 10 p.m.

"I kept going to college, finished my master's and went on to my first semester towards my Ph.D., when suddenly, I realized I was overwhelmed. There wasn't enough of me to go around."

Her house had sold, her divorce was final, and she couldn't find an affordable, safe place to live.

"In court, during the divorce settlement process, the judge said my husband only had to pay $300 a month," Sally says. "I stood up and said, 'Your honor, I understand that Delaware is a dual support state, and there's nothing I want to do more than care for my children, but if you think $300 a month is half of what it takes to support a family, you are wrong. He answered that he only asked fathers to pay a small amount, because if it were more, the fathers wouldn't pay at all. I thought this was an incredibly sexist remark."

Sally was furious, but the judgment stood, and it made her chances of finding a nice place to live with her children more difficult. She saw a newspaper ad for a house to rent in Hockessin

"I made an appointment to see it, and it was perfect," says Sally. "The man looked at me and my sons and said, 'Where is your husband?' I told him this was my family and he said, 'I'm sorry, but I think the house has already been rented.'"

The next day, in the grocery store, she ran into the owner of the real estate agency that was renting the home. "I thought to myself, *Okay, God has put this man right in your path so seize the moment!* I waited until he got into line, and then slipped in behind him. He said, 'Oh, Mrs. Coons, I see your house sold.' 'Yes it did', I said. He asked where we were going to move. And I said, 'Funny you should ask that.' Next thing I knew, I was renting the house."

"A colleague and I were hired to set up a new program in the school district for teens who had been expelled from high school for violent behavior," says Sally. "The truth of the matter is, if you expel a young person when he or she is 14, 15 or 16, chances are he or she will never go back to high school and ultimately have difficulty with employment."

Sally and her colleague developed an approach to teaching English, math and science that held the kids' interest. She learned that if children don't read well by the time they leave the third grade, the chances are high they'll face many lifelong difficulties. She was making a positive impact. Her job was satisfying, and she was reveling in raising her kids. Life was good, and it was about to get better.

"I met my second husband, Bob, at a party," says Sally. "We married seven months later, rented a house in Hockessin for a couple of years, then built a house."

The "Bob" whom Sally is referring to is Robert W. Gore, chairman of the board of W. L. Gore & Associates, Inc. which is best known as the developer of waterproof, breathable GORE-TEX® fabric.

After settling into their new home, Sally went to work for W. L. Gore & Associates, Inc. in what she describes as a "non-descript kind of job."

"Bob suggested I take a look at Gore's employee benefits, because he didn't think they were very competitive," Sally says. "I ended up creating and organizing a human resources department with about 100 people worldwide in China, Japan, Germany, Italy,

United Kingdom, and Scotland as well as the USA. Of course, I knew nothing about the field of human resources going in. I just did it, and had a wonderful time doing it. It was a fabulous 25 years."

Sally retired in 2005 from Gore, but not from the work she truly was born to do: rolling up her societal sleeves, helping people live better lives, and finding solutions to difficult problems.

"I'm involved with many organizations," she says. "With the help of my son, Chris, I founded Vision to Learn, which brings eye glasses to children at school so they can, at last, see what they're doing. We outfitted a Mercedes van, which visits each school. Classroom by classroom, the children who have been examined by the school nurse go out to the van. The optometrist in the van examines each child, and then the optician, also there, fits them for glasses which are delivered to them two weeks later. They get to pick their own frames—there are pink ones, and some with sparkles in them. The kids are thrilled to be able to see correctly!"

Sally's Final Thoughts

There are resources out there, and you can find them. Learn to ask for help. Don't give up. Eventually, you will find someone who will say, "I can help."

Keep the faith and remember that you are a good person and God is looking out for you.

Anne T. Hogan

Anne T. Hogan

"If I can paraglide in New Zealand, I can do anything!"

Biography

Anne T. Hogan is chief executive officer of the Girl Scouts of the Chesapeake Bay (GSCB), the Delmarva Peninsula's premiere organization for girls, encompassing more than 16,500 girl and adult members in the state of Delaware, the Eastern Shore of Maryland, and the Eastern Shore of Virginia.

Anne has been involved in girl scouting since she was seven years old. While growing up in Massachusetts and through a three-decade career in the banking industry, Anne continued her involvement as a volunteer leader and as president of the Massachusetts-based Spar and Spindle Girl Scout Council's board of directors. After moving to Delaware in 1991, she joined the board of the Girl Scouts of the Chesapeake Bay.

She credits the Girl Scouts for teaching her core skills such as responsibility, respect and integrity, which influenced her success as a corporate executive. As senior executive vice president and director of portfolio marketing operations at MBNA, those skills helped her launch the bank's global operations in the U.K. and manage 500 employees.

Since becoming GSCB's chief executive officer in 2008, Anne has overseen the construction of the Lynn W. Williams Science and Technology Lodge, the first building in Delaware to earn Platinum Certification for Leadership in Energy and Environmental Design (LEED). She and her team celebrated the 100th anniversary of the Girl Scouts and the 50th anniversary of the council with special events throughout the year. They included a birthday celebration with 1,400 girls and adults; the 13th annual Women of Distinction celebration, an exhibition at the Delaware History Museum; and the national launch of The Year of the Girl.

Anne encourages other professional women to consider volunteering their time with Girl Scouts.

Anne's Story

A female friend told me that having been a Girl Scout when she was young was one of the most significant and memorable experiences of her life. She didn't remember a much about other parts of her childhood, but her Girl Scout memories remain vivid. I asked her why.

"I think it's because many of the skills I learned in Girl Scouts are with me to this day," she said. "Each time I go camping with the kids and we toast marshmallows on long sticks over the campfire to make s'mores, I think of my days at Girl Scout camp making sit---upons (homemade waterproof cushions), and washing my mess kit and hanging it to dry in homemade mesh bags. I remember gathering kindling in the woods for making a fire, learning how to identify poison ivy, and diving into an icy mountain lake to learn to swim. When I crochet or knit afghans during winter, I think of the sweet troop leader who taught me to cast on stitches. My Girl Scout green sash was filled with badges, each representing the achievement of a goal. I sewed them on myself with a needle and green thread, so each time I sew on a button, I think of the Girls Scouts."

It made me wonder how girls might remember the sweet face of Anne T. Hogan, who has devoted more than 40 years to the Girls Scouts. She has personally, and through her leadership, touched the lives of thousands of young girls. She's made a tremendous impact in the world. She talks funny, too, like the exaggerated, *"Pahk yah cah in Hahvahd yahd. (Park your car in Harvard Yard, to the rest of us.)*

She was born in Salem, Mass., near Gallows Hill, the site of the Witch Trial Hangings in 1692. Her parents, Rita and James Hogan, were also born there. She is the oldest of four siblings.

"My parents grew up together, but went their separate ways after high school," says Anne. "When Mom was 17, she joined the Women's Army Corps, much to her mother's dismay."

Meanwhile, Anne's father went to Canada to study to be a priest, but something made him change his mind. "I think he always had a thing for my mother," Anne explains, "so he came back, joined the Navy, married her, and I came along a few years later."

Anne describes her mother as fun and well liked. "She was outgoing, always bubbly and constantly taking us places. But when I was 11, she got breast cancer."

As her illness progressed, Anne's mother, who had worked as an X-ray technician, moved to the hospital across the street. Anne, the oldest child, helped her father with household chores and cared for her siblings.

"I made four, brown bag lunches, ironed two white shirts and two peter pan collars for our school uniform every night," says Anne. "I didn't mind a bit. I was also a Candy Striper at the hospital. You were able to do a lot more then as compared to what you're allowed to do now."

Anne's father took care of his wife. It was the couple's tradition to have a Scotch and water together before dinner to discuss the day's events. He continued the tradition by bringing her the cocktail every night after work.

"I adored my father and wanted to help as much as I could," Anne says. "We were very close. When I was 13, I skipped school and helped him buy Christmas presents." Anne's mother passed away on January 28th, shortly after Anne's 14th birthday.

Anne's memories of her mother grew faint over the years. She wishes she could remember more, but there are pleasant snapshots. "She was a woman who rolled up her sleeves and got things done," says Anne. "And she knew how to get everyone on board. She laughed a lot. I remember her being a good listener, and she didn't beat around the bush."

At her mother's urging Anne became a Girl Scout at eight. Her aunt and a neighbor were troop leaders. She considers herself a "walking commercial" for the Girl Scouts. It was the outlet she needed.

"I went camping every year in Maine for two weeks," she recalls. "I have friends to this day from that camp. I remember learning first aid and sewing. To earn my sewing badge, I sewed onto a piece of material two eyes, a nose and buttons for the mouth. After that I was able to sew on my own badges. I even earned a Good Housekeeping badge!"

It was also during high school that Anne had thoughts of becoming an astronaut. She wrote to NASA in Houston to get all the information she could. Her school projects even involved space travel.

"Do you remember Sputnik?" she says. "I remember being in our den, folding clothes, watching on a little black-and-white TV the astronaut coming down the ladder on the moon. I think my interest waned, however, when I realized being an astronaut involved the study of engineering."

Thank to her mom, Anne never thought that there would be any restrictions in life because of being a woman.

"My mother was ahead of her time," says Anne. "She was a golfer and a good athlete. We didn't have much traffic on our street when we were kids, so we'd play baseball. My mother pitched and we'd hit. She'd say, 'If you love something, just do it.' My father told us the same thing."

If anything held Anne back, it was giving up things she loved to do. Her father was away often on sales trips so she was responsible for her siblings.

"One time, as the Sophomore Class President, I organized a horseback riding event," she recalls. "But when the time came to go I was needed to stay home and take care of things there. But it was fine, my dad needed my help so I didn't mind."

Anne's father remarried when she was in high school. "His new wife, Nora, loved him enough to move 75 miles from her home to a house with four kids.

My dad was my biggest strength and support. I suppose every daughter thinks her dad is wonderful, but mine really was. Unfortunately, he died at 57 from Lou Gehrig's Disease."

Anne considers herself a cheerleader for Girl Scouts. "I went all the way through (the Scout ranks) and finished when I was 18. I earned the Gold Award, which was a big deal at the time. Less than five percent of girls receive the Gold Award. Girl Scouts planted in me the urge to travel and have fun adventures."

Anne went to St. James, an all girls Catholic school in Salem. She had loads of fun but was a bit of a troublemaker. "My lab partner and I almost blew up the chemistry classroom," she laughs. "Dottie, who is now a senior nurse, wasn't paying attention to the Bunsen burner, and bingo! There was an explosion. I distinctly remember that the chemistry lab was brand new. I ran out screaming, thinking my father was going to kill me."

Then there was the time Anne's class traveled to the United Nations in New York as the culmination of a school project. "We were each assigned to contact a person from a foreign country and collect information," she says. "My contact was a man from Guyana, and he invited us to lunch in the dining room for special guests of the delegates. Everything was great until he ordered pig's feet for everyone, with a special sauce. I was mortified, but I took a bite because I had been raised to do so. He could tell I didn't like it, but he was very gracious."

After earning an associate degree, Anne went to work as a bank teller. After a few years, a friend who lived in Minneapolis, Minn., suggested she join her there and become roommates. Anne lived in Minnesota for five years while working as an accounting manager for a bank, but took a leave and returned home when her father became ill.

"My brother drove back with me from Minneapolis," Anne says. "We drove to Hampton Beach, N.H. to our family cottage, which is where my father was. It was July, and hotter than heck. My dad was in a wheelchair and couldn't speak. A couple days later, he got pneumonia, so we took him back to Salem. He died about three weeks later."

Anne stayed with her stepmother, Nora, who was heartbroken at the loss of her husband. "I didn't want to leave her alone," Anne says, "but one night, a friend invited me to the movies. When I got back, there was an ambulance in front of the house. My Aunt, who lived downstairs had had a massive heart attack and I was the executor of the estate. I let my boss in Minneapolis know that I wouldn't be coming back, and got a job as the operations manager at a Salem bank."

A relative who had known and admired Anne's mother visited whenever he was in town. His name was Charles Cawley, a founding member of MBNA (which was sold to Bank of America in 2006). Anne says he was a wonderful man.

"He invited me to visit him at MBNA in Wilmington once," says Anne. "Nora went with me. He introduced me to many individuals including the senior operating committee and asked for my thoughts. 'There aren't any women,' I said. Ultimately, I was invited to work there.

"I started as an assistant vice president and was promoted," she adds. "Who would have ever thought I'd be a banker? It's still amazing to me."

Anne was selected to participate with 24 other people company wide to participate in their "Marketing Excellence" training, a very intense, four-month program. Afterwards, Anne was asked to go to England to help get a new bank and its credit department up and running.

"I was honored to be one of six executives who were selected," she says. "We were the bank's first Senior Operating Committee, and I was the only woman. One night, I was invited to attend a dinner in the Parliament's dining room. I was one of four women out of maybe 75 men."

Anne was directed to sit with Sir Jeffrey Archer, a Member of Parliament who subsequently became a best selling novelist.

"He was very cordial," Anne says. "He spent the whole evening talking to me. He wanted to know all about my American bank, MBNA, what our business was exactly, how we selected our staff and how we treated them. He wanted to know how we treated our customers, because the American way of doing things was very different than the British way. He grilled me, then commended me afterwards for being able to hold my own with him."

The fact that MBNA, an American bank that had come to England to set up a credit department in a country that didn't yet have a credit bureau system, fascinated the British public and the bank was featured in many of the English newspapers. The buzz caught the attention of another British notable—Charles, Prince of Wales.

"Prince Charles was very interested in architecture and he wanted to visit the new American bank," Anne says. "As you can imagine we dusted and polished everything, preparing for his visit. I was in a classroom where the credit analysts were being trained, and in walked Prince Charles. He walked right up to me, shook my hand, asked me lots of questions about myself, i.e., my name, who I was, and what I did. Then he asked what all the people were doing in that classroom. After five or six minutes, he very nicely apologized for interrupting the class, shook my hand again, and left. Aside from our CEO and his assistant, I believe I was the only other person he spoke with that day."

The moment Prince Charles left, Anne says, everyone got their phones out and called their mothers.

"MBNA became a very big deal there," she says. "I was there five and a half years, and when I left, we were the second largest credit card issuer in England. It was amazing how lucky I was, first to be selected to go, promoted several times, and then to be appointed as one of six members of the first European Senior Operating Committee."

Anne says it took a little time to get adjusted to the British way of life. The MBNA banks there were open at 9 a.m. to 3 p.m. on weekdays and closed on Saturdays. Grocery stores closed at 5 p.m. and were open until noon on Saturdays.

"There was quite a bit to get used to," says Anne. "I couldn't get tuna fish in a can, for instance. But in the five-and-a-half years that I was there, the banks changed hours to reflect what we're used to in America, and grocery stores stayed open 24 hours. And, finally, people started accepting that I was a senior officer at the bank."

Anne made many friends, went to shows, and took in an air tour every other weekend. "Brits take a month off in January, February or March," she explains. "Air Tours had a wonderful program where you could pay £99 and go to Rome or Florence for the day. They had all kinds of trips, and I signed up for every one of them. I was so fortunate to go all over Europe, which felt adventurous to me."

Anne was at MBNA for 15 years, serving as senior executive vice president, before Bank of America acquired it in 2006.

"I've had a place in Naples, Fla., for several years," Anne says. "My last day at the bank was in November. On January 1, I drove down to Naples and stayed there for a year. Golfing and sitting on the beach was great, and for those first few months it was what I needed, but I began to get the itch to do something."

Before leaving for Naples, Anne accompanied her brother to China to pick up the little girl that he and his wife had adopted. On the plane back home, while her brother slept, Anne and the baby drew pictures with crayons.

"My little brother (the youngest sibling) and I have always been close," Anne says. "He now has Lou Gehrig's disease. He and his wife are wonderful. They call me 'auntie.' That little girl is now a freshman in high school. She's outstanding and has been a wonderful addition to our family. They named her Catherine which had been my mother's middle name."

Upon her return to the United States, Anne joined the Girl Scouts' Board of Directors. "CEO Judy Taggart called me and invited me to take her position when she retired, and though my first response was, 'Are you kidding me? No thanks,' I thought about it," Anne says. "I flew up to meet with her. She showed me her calendar—when it got busy, when camp started—and I decided to apply. There were 87 people across the country who applied!"

Anne was required to write a business plan, something she hadn't done in years. The field was narrowed down to 10 finalists, and then two.

"I flew back for the Women of Distinction event, and two days later met the staff," she says. "They called me to tell me I'd gotten the job. For me, it was like having come full circle, and it was deeply satisfying to know that I was in a position where I could make a difference for girls."

Anne was never married. "There have been men in my life, wonderful guys, but not one with whom I felt that special connection," she says. "I was fine being a single woman because I was able to have a good life and make a difference.

"I have been so blessed, traveling, experiencing new things," she says. "If I can paraglide in New Zealand, I can do anything!"

Anne's Final Thoughts

This is what I say to my girls: Believe in yourself. Don't stop trying. Don't accept no as a final answer. Be proud, be yourself, and be happy at what you do.

Robin Horn, M. D.

Robin Horn, M.D.

"Life keeps changing, so you have to change with it. I'm always digging in and trying to learn new things."

Biography

Robin Horn became a Medical Doctor in 1989. After medical school, she left the east coast to go to University of Michigan for her residency in Internal Medicine. While there she became enamored with cardiology. She stayed on for a one year after her residency for a combined academic appointment at the VA Medical Center and University of Michigan Medical Center.

In 1993, she began her four-year fellowship at the Mayo Clinic. Her area of interest is in non-invasive cardiology with a focus in echocardiography and nuclear medicine. She was elected to be Mayo Clinic fellow representative at the American College of Cardiology in 1997 in a special forum for fellows in training.

Upon graduation, she returned to her roots and joined a private cardiology practice in Delaware. Given her extensive background in non-invasive cardiology, Robin was immediately recruited to the committee responsible for quality control in diagnostic testing. In 2009, she was asked to become lab director for echocardiography and nuclear medicine and help to oversee the vascular work being done as well.

In the early years, she was elected to executive physician leadership of the group. This is an elected position for a two-year term. She has been elected to serve as part of the executive leadership team for 12 years.

In 2011, the private practice group merged with Christiana Care. She still practices today with the same cardiology group. After full merger of the Christiana inpatient lab with the outpatient labs she was promoted to co-director of the non-invasive lab at Christiana Care. She participates in lab accreditation, actively leads and directs nurse practitioners in the performance of cardiac stress tests, and directs sonographers and physicians in providing quality studies and interpretations in echocardiography, nuclear and vascular imaging.

85

Robin's Story

The first time I heard Robin Horn speak was at a Mid-Atlantic Women's conference at the University of Delaware. She was excellent, informative, very comfortable and professional in her presentation. I liked her instantly! She was warm and funny and not pretentious. There were 200 women in the room and only one man—me.

She and I got to talking, and she confessed that she liked to dance, and doesn't care if she doesn't "look pretty" while doing it, because, she said, dancing is her freedom, and she doesn't have to be tipsy to do it.

I liked her so much I put her on my "music room party" invitee list and she and her husband came and "danced the night away" to the music of Club Phred.

Since then, I asked her to speak at a Newark Morning Rotary Club meeting about "Heart Disease," and her presentation was met with resounding applause and laughter. We have a great Rotary Club that encourages "fun," and she gave as good as she got. They loved her.

Robin was born in Wilmington, Del. to Joanne and Al Horn. She is the youngest of three children, all born within a year of each other—Irish triplets, she calls them. Debbie, the oldest, is an accountant who owns several farm stands in Maryland, and Bryan, who she describes as "tall and charming," is in sales and marketing and lives in California.

"My mother couldn't figure out why she kept getting pregnant," Robin says, "and she used to say, 'Let me tell you—the rhythm method doesn't work.'"

Robin says her mother had a tremendous, positive impact on her. "She always said, 'Don't settle for less!' Her father, my grandfather, had said things like, 'Women need to be barefoot and pregnant. Why do you need to educate yourself?' She left home at the age of 18, married my father, had three children, and then decided she was going to advance in her career. She started as a secretary and worked toward a college degree, paying the tuition with my father's help."

Robin's father worked nights in gas stations so that he could be home during the day and take care of the kids while her mother attended classes. Then, when her mother graduated with a degree in chemistry, they switched roles. Joanne took care of the kids while Al attended vocational school to study heating and air conditioning, and worked odd jobs so the family could get ahead.

"Mom worked hard at her career," Robin says. "Eventually, she had a job managing trademarks, which was unheard of for someone who didn't have anything but an undergraduate degree in chemistry. When my sister started college, Mom put herself through law school. By the time I was in college, there was a year when everyone in our family was in school, except for my Dad, and he survived!"

Robin says her mother doesn't view herself as successful. Rather, she sees herself as someone who came from nothing and achieved her goals.

"When I talked with my mother about what I was going to do with my life, I told her I wanted something in the science field, but with a caring role," Robin says. "I mentioned nursing school and my mother said, 'Why do you want to be a nurse, when you could be a doctor?' She was the pusher behind the scenes, but she was also a giver. She'd give us giant hugs, too much food and the most loving support when we fell down. 'Get up,' she'd say. 'Get up and try again.'"

In sharp contract, Robin's father was calm, off to the side, watching and smiling.

"He always said, 'Don't take life too seriously,'" says Robin. 'Make sure you laugh. Your mother's right—get an education so you won't have to do what I do. Get ahead, but take a moment to laugh. Take a step back. Don't beat yourself up too hard. Yup, you locked your key in your car today. Not everything turns out the way you want.'"

Robin grew up in an era when kids played outside. There was no fear of abduction, she says, because she was always with her brother and sister or friends.

"I can remember all of the mothers coming outside when it was beginning to get dark outside," she recalls. "I remember playing in the pool at Hercules Country Club, playing Matchbox cars with my brother, or riding bikes. My parents were very busy and often couldn't drive us anywhere, so I remember, as a teenager, riding my bike from Newark to Hockessin, without thinking anything of it. I must have been in great shape."

When she was 13, Robin got to host a Panamanian student as part of her high school's foreign exchange program.

"I wanted it so badly," she says. "My mother says I absolutely drove her nuts. I don't remember that part—but I remember being incredibly interested in all things international, and I loved languages. We hosted a student in our home for six weeks, and my brother was supposed to take care of him, but he wasn't really interested, so I got to take the guy to my classroom."

When she was 14, Robin got to travel to Panama as an exchange student, and it changed her life.

"At our house, Mom gave us chores, and when our chores were done we could go outside and play," says Robin. "Mom believed that kids should be allowed to be kids. But the expectations of my host family were quite different. They had a farm. Girls were expected to work all day, keep the kitchens going, and clean. Basically, we went to school, did chores, did homework, then went to bed. The host mother and I didn't really hit it off, mostly because of the language barrier. I went back the next year and stayed with a family with parents more like my own. Once the day's work was done, we were free to be kids."

Robin was struck by the many lifestyle and cultural differences.

"There wasn't a lot of wealth, so there people living in shacks," she says. "Not everyone had shoes. I ate a lot of rice and beans, because the meat there is so tough. It made me realize how lucky I was, so lucky. My parents worked very hard to keep up, but still, we had everything we needed. I think realizing this helped me to develop character. I'll work with anyone, because not everyone is educated, has means, or understands your language."

Another childhood experience that strongly influenced Robin's character and world view was when her mother decided she wanted to learn to ski. Robin doesn't remember how old she was—perhaps early teens—but it happened in Vermont.

"We'd stay at Misty Mountain Lodge for a week at a time," she says. "Then one day, my parents announced they'd bought acres of land and we, as a family, were going to build a house. Literally, the five of us were going to build it. My mother said that the only way we could keep skiing was to build a house of our own. Over the next year, we spent 40 out of 52 weekends building that house. They still own that property ."

Robin thought her parents were insane, but it gave her a strong work ethic, almost as strong as her father's.

"My father lives and breathes work," Robin explains. "Even to this day. His idea of fun is to go work in the yard, do major cleanups. My mother finally convinced him that at his age he should hire someone else to do it. Still, he goes out there and works with them. He doesn't like to just let somebody come in and do all the work."

Robin's mother taught her about what a woman's role ought to be in society by telling stories from her own experiences.

"A law firm she worked for used to give the *Wall Street Journal* to their attorneys, who were men," she says, "but when my mother got hired, she didn't get one. The guys would always invite each other to luncheons and not include my mother. She advised us to always strive to get ahead and look out for ourselves, but to be careful how we did it. She's a very strong-willed person who smashed a lot of egos, and has some regrets about that."

Robin says she was a good student and able to do well in school. Her problem was trying to figure out what she was going to do in life.

"I just knew I wanted to do something important," she says. "I didn't want to be an Olympic athlete or President of the United States, just something that mattered, and in which, in my mother's eyes, I'd be able to make a living. Nowadays, kids learn that they're visual or auditory learners. There was none of that when I was in school, no breaking down academics according to how a person learned. My best friend and I would study for and take the same science test. She'd get a C, and I'd get an A. It was heartbreaking, because she's very smart and extremely verbal."

Robin earned a bachelor's degree in chemistry at the University of Delaware and a masters in physiology from Hahnemann University. After that, she went to Boston for her M.D., and then to Ann Arbor for her residency.

"School got harder for me after high school," Robin says. "It wasn't intuitive anymore. My statistics class in grad school was particularly difficult. I'd come through calculus, so I felt I'd get through this, too, but I was worried. Fortunately, a guy who owned a computer company helped me break it down into a language I could understand. I worked for him part time so I could earn some extra money."

Robin's parents paid for her first four years of college, and she paid for graduate and medical schools. She did data entry, set up and cleaned labs, and worked as a waitress at a place called Legal Seafood in Boston Commons.

Robin's husband of 20 years, Mark, is a nurse practitioner in trauma, and for that reason, Robin strongly recommends that Mark and I never meet—professionally, that is. The two met at the University of Michigan in Ann Arbor. He was a nurse, and she was a resident.

"He kept trying to talk to me all the time," she says. "It was bugging me. You see, when I'm at work, I'm very busy and preoccupied. It's not that I'm unfriendly—just the opposite. I wanted to befriend people, and I'd greet people in the halls and comment on their nice nails or ask if they had any Oreo cookies, and it made the shift go much better. But Mark was persistent about talking to me, asking how I was, or whether there was anything he could do for me, or tell me I needed to eat better because I kept raiding the cookie jar. I didn't want to stop and chat. I wanted to keep moving."

One night, Mark, who is an avid sailor, attended one of Robin's lectures. He waited until the members of the audience had finished talking to her, and invited her to coffee.

"And then, I realized that he wasn't trying to bug me. He liked me!" she says. "He's so supportive. He reminds me to stay in the game. He may complain that my hours are long, but he's the first person to stand behind me."

Robin describes her leadership style as that of being a role model. She prefers to lead by example, rather than trying to take control of an entire room.

"I take charge in the lecture setting," she says. "Funny thing is, I never thought I was that good of a speaker. I was forcibly videotaped when I was in residency. I prefer to be quietly determined and go along, not to be center stage. That's my personality style. Then, I looked at myself, and thought, 'I'm not *that* bad.' Then, the instructor told everyone in my group that I was the best, and I realized I could speak after all."

It became Robin's turn to give "grand rounds." This is the part of medical training when a student must present the medical problems and treatment of a patient to a group of doctors, residents and medical students.

"I prepped and prepped," she recalls. "I watched videos of people I liked. I didn't want to be boring, like so many lecturers are. I decided I was going to imitate some of the ones I liked, where they would walk back and forth on the stage and engage the audience. The feedback I got was off the charts. I wasn't looking to be a leader in that regard, but it led to me doing a lot of public speaking."

Robin was invited by Christiana Care Health System to do a "Women in Cardiology" series, and she gladly agreed, even though it paid nothing and had to be scheduled in her personal time. At the first talk, 50 people showed up, and husband Mark helped her with the hand-outs. She did many talks, and although she was tired at times, she didn't shirk.

"People were so appreciative that it made the hard work worthwhile," said Robin. "Sometimes I'd say to myself, 'Why am I here? I have kids. I have a family, and a life.' But then, people would come up to me afterwards, and one after the other would say, 'Thank you so much.' I think it's because my talks help people make more informed decisions, and I'm someone they feel they can trust to be honest with them."

Robin says she doesn't have any hobbies, per se, other than raising her children and playing the piano. Robin has two 19-year-old daughters, who are fraternal twins. Kelsey is a field hockey player and Breanna is a musician. Robin is a devoted mother who has always made it a high priority to go to her daughters' events.

"My girls are wonderful," she says. "You'd like them. As for my dog, a bichon, that's a different story. Her name is Angel. She's adorable, but she's not angelic. We don't leave the trash out, for example, and she takes the toilet paper, chews it up, then stands next to it with pride. Quite the charmer!"

Robin had to make many sacrifices during her career, but her mother's admonition to make good choices has been a compass that guides her through the biggest challenges.

"People who go into healthcare know that they're going to have to make sacrifices," says Robin. "When we're on call, we miss holidays, and we have to accept that. If I have to work 4th of July, Memorial Day or Labor Day, it's no problem. We'd celebrate on a different day and have just as much fun."

Robin's Final Thoughts

Choose what's important to you, and don't give up. You have to dig in a lot of times. If you want family and career, you have to choose what's important. Choose whether you're going to clean the house or go to the ball game. Most times, you can't do both.

When you make choices, people are going to challenge you, more by women than by men. My closest girlfriends don't challenge me, and they are not in healthcare. They support and applaud me. It's totally amazing.

As for the women who challenge me, I say to them, "Be careful how much you bring down other women. We need to support each other."

We are not our parents, who lived in the generation when Mom would work a job, come home and cook the meals. In today's world, if you're not a single parent, you aren't forced to do that, because husbands are chipping in more. Life keeps changing, so you have to change with it. I'm always digging in and trying to learn new things.

Do whatever comes along in your career, even if it's not what you think you want. Follow the lead. When I was invited to speak more and more often to women, I was afraid I'd be put into that box. I didn't want to be a doctor only for women. I wanted to be a doctor for everybody. But now, years later, I see that everything's perfect and I'm able to make a difference.

Susan Hum

Susan Hum

"Your legacy is the sum of all your achievements."

Biography

Susan Hum is a costume designer who worked with David Letterman for more than 32 years, starting with "Late Night with David Letterman" (NBC-TV, 1984-93) and "Late Show with David Letterman" (CBS-TV, 1993-2015).

Susan estimates she designed more than 300 single and double-breasted suits for Letterman, and bought at least 500 of his designer ties. For many years, Letterman made the New York papers as the best-dressed talk show host on television.

She also was the creative mind behind hundreds of outrageous sometimes bizarre, but always hilarious costumes that best friends of the Late Show Bill Murray and Bruce Willis wore making many appearances doing comedy skits.

As the writers would have it, Susan appeared in many episodes interrupting Letterman's monologue.

Her lifetime professional experience includes costume design for live television, soap operas, commercials, music videos, movies and theatre.

Born in Louisville, Ky. and raised on a farm in Landenberg, Pa., Susan graduated from Kennett High School and with a degree in art education from the Moore College of Art & Design in Philadelphia. During the early years of her career, she worked as an art teacher in Binghamton, N.Y. and Copiague, N.Y. and later pursued a full-time career in costume design after some early successes in the New York theatre scene, in productions such as "Spoon River Anthology," (1970), "The Year of the Dragon," playwright Frank Chin (1974), and many more.

Other work includes commercials for Sony, New York Lotto, Maxwell House and other distinguished national brands. In television, Susan's credits include the "Miss America Pageant," "Miss Teen American Pageant," "The Guiding Light," "Another World," and "The Doctors."

Susan's Story

The creative and accomplished Susan Hum and I have an enduring friendship that began many years ago when her father, Chang L. Hum, was in the early stages of his struggle with dementia.

My wife, Louise, and I met Chang at a Sunday brunch at the church we'd just joined. He was a brilliant, extraordinary man with whom we fell instantly in love, and we were delighted when he invited us back to his home so that we could further our acquaintance.

As we drove behind his car, we noticed that Chang was driving randomly, as if he was lost. As it turns out, he *was* lost, but at last, we arrived at his house, and it appeared he was living alone.

"Do you have any children?" I asked. "Is there one with whom you are particularly close? I'd like to give them a call and tell them you're okay."

Chang gave me the phone number of his daughter, Susan, who lived in New York. I called her and said, "I'm here with your dad in the kitchen. He's ok but I think he's having some challenges and maybe it's time to check in on him more closely to see if there's something you can do to help him."

To Susan's credit, she dropped everything and made a beeline to her father's farm in Landenberg. She visited him every weekend for six months until it became necessary for her father to move in with her in Brooklyn. Louise and I frequently joined them for dinner on the farm when they would come for the weekends. Susan became well acquainted with Chang's church friends and she took lots of Polaroid pictures so that her father would have something to remember of the people and places he loved. She was terrific.

It's worth mentioning that for the longest time, I had no idea what Susan did for a living. When talking about work, she'd simply say, "My company did this, or my company wouldn't let me do that." I finally asked, "Where do you work?" Without the slightest affectation, she said, "Oh, I'm Dave Letterman's costume designer, going on 20 years now."

Dave's first nighttime talk show on NBC TV was "Late Night" with David Letterman," and he usually wore a sport coat, simple tie, Wigwam white wool sweat socks, baggy Girbaud beige pants and wrestling shoes. When this show ended, he moved over to CBS and wanted to spruce up his image by wearing nicer suits.

Susan bought designer foulard and striped ties, and chose the tailor for his suits, typically six to two-button double-breasted suits. Susan made decisions on the choice of fabrics best suited for style and what looked good on camera. He also wore Cole Haan loafers and light grey custom made knee socks by GoldToe. Off camera, says Susan, "he was very casual, wearing sneakers, jeans, shorts and a tee shirt."

Susan is also known for the creation of numerous outrageous comedic crazy costumes (upon last-minute instructions from the writers), such as the human cheese dip suit, Velcro jumpsuit, rice crispy suit, suit of magnets and the marshmallow suit which was set on fire with blowtorches. Susan spent many all-nighters putting these costumes together.

Susan's father, Chang, was a civil engineer, born in the rural Kwangtung province of China. Her mother, Mary, was born in Chinatown in New York City.

"I don't know a whole lot about my mother's Asian heritage," Susan says, "because I think it's an Asian thing, not talking. Being immigrants, their focus was on the present, working hard to provide and achieve their goal, the American Dream, for a better life and education for their children."

Susan's mother, Mary, was one of two daughters and three brothers. Susan doesn't know the details, but Mary's sister died as a child, which took an emotional toll. Mary was the oldest of the siblings, so she essentially raised and cared for her brothers. She was the main person in the family who could speak English. It was difficult for her, having two parents not knowing the English language, and experiencing prejudice toward the Asian population during World War II.

"Trying to bridge the cultures was hard for my mother," says Susan. "Her mother had bound feet, as was the custom in wealthy Hong Kong families. It was arranged that she be shipped off to the U.S. to marry my grandfather, so I assume the families knew each other in Hong Kong."

Mary grew up working in her father's Chinese restaurant, The Far East Restaurant, on Delaware Avenue in Wilmington, Del.

"My mother was ambitious," says Susan, and she furthered her education by attending Goldey-Beacom College. My parents married just before World War II. My father enlisted in the Army, since he took ROTC at University of Delaware. This left my mother on her own raising two toddlers and one infant daughter.

Chang came to the United States on his own in 1928 at 18 to get an engineering degree at the University of Delaware. He intended to get his degree and return to China. Susan says he was a boarder at the YMCA in Wilmington, which was across the street from The Far East Restaurant, where the future Mrs. Hum worked.

At the YMCA, Chang met Francis Clark, a board member and philanthropist with a master's degree in Asian Studies. Clark took young Chang under his wing and sent him to Mount Hermon, a private secondary school in Massachusetts, to assimilate and learn English. Afterwards, during World War II, Chang served as a Captain in the armed forces behind enemy lines, making shipments of grain on both the Yellow and Yangtze Rivers.

"I know my father was with Brigadier General Stillwell 7th Infantry China Burma India Theater, Susan says. When film producer and writer Ed Burns was a guest on the Letterman Show, I happened to have brief conversation with him. He had made a documentary about Asian World War II veterans. I mentioned to Ed that my father was unwilling to talk about the war, and Ed said it was hard to get info from that generation because culturally, they didn't talk about their past."

Chang received a degree in civil engineering at University of Delaware. When World War II ended, his first engineering job was with DuPont. His next job was with The Hercules Powder Company as a structural engineer where he became the head of the engineering department. He was credited with a group of engineers for the construction of the Delaware Memorial Bridge, Hercules plants and also worked on satellite stands for USA space projects.

"In 1949, my father moved the family from Wilmington to a 60-acre farm he'd purchased in Landenberg, Pa.," Susan says. "The fieldstone house had some electricity, an outhouse, and an old hand pump that drew water from a spring in the basement. He named it Kemlan Farms. It was his dream, owning a farm."

Chang remodeled the entire house and added two additions. Susan says she was his right hand man with home repairs and farm work. But the house wasn't their only pioneer living experience.

"In elementary school, I went to two, one-room school houses with outhouses, coal burning stoves for heat and water pumped from outdoor wells," she recalls. "There was one scary teacher who taught three grades. I was a very shy child who was afraid to speak."

Susan says first generation Asian parents were very strict disciplinarians, sometimes going above and beyond. There were always chores to do on a working farm. With her two sisters and brother, Susan fed the cows every morning before school, cleaned out the barn, and, with her siblings, helped her father fence the entire property.

"I found out later that our Black Angus herd paid for everyone's college educations," Susan says, "One year, when I was about 14, we had a poor crop of corn, probably from a drought. We spent every weekend in the corn field that Fall, harvesting seven acres of field corn by hand."

Chang farmed the property while working full time at his day job. "At the beginning of spring, at night, you could see the tractor lights traveling back and forth across the land, plowing the field. I would till the field and rake the hay in rows with our 1950's Ford tractor to get ready for the hay baler.

"My mother was the proverbial Tiger Mom, in the old traditional Chinese style," Susan says. "She had a lot of determination, which may be the result of a difficult immigrant upbringing, and having been treated as a second class citizen, having been born a female in a Chinese patriarchal society. She became an accomplished landscape watercolor artist, sewed beautiful dresses and knitted incredible sweaters for her daughters and herself. On top of that, she landscaped the gardens around the house and had an enormous knowledge of tree and plants. I learned how to cook all the Chinese dishes from my mother."

Susan's mother ruled the household, and some of her disciplinary actions were harsh.

"There was an enormous amount of psychological household stress from my mother's never---ending commands and criticism," says Susan. "I feel that the stern childhood robbed us kids of our identities. We had to find our way through life with limited social skills. Our family was totally isolated on the farm. There were no other Asian families nearby. It was a clash of cultures. My parents held fast to Chinese traditional values while wanting us to grow up as Americans. My parents never taught us the Chinese language. As a family, we pretty much stayed to ourselves. Going to school and being involved in activities was our only outside connection to the community."

Susan discovered she had a talent for drawing, and it helped her escape mentally.

"Drawing was my only source of self-esteem, which teachers noticed through all my school years," she says. "Other sources of strength were being close to my sisters and my dog, being in touch with nature and the cows, and going to my secret place in the woods where this beautiful Dogwood tree stood in a clearing in a pool of sunshine. I see now that there was a message in all my parents' madness. Their goal in life was to raise their children on a farm away from the city, away from prejudice, getting a good education and learning the value of hard work so that we could achieve the American life style."

In her senior year of high school, Susan heard about Saturday art classes at Moore College of Art in Philadelphia. She wanted to be a fashion designer.

"My parents decided I would major in art education for job security, or else, no college," Susan says. "Of course I went along, because college was the big step to freedom. I attended Moore College of Art on a senatorial scholarship getting a bachelor's degree in art education. Those four years living in the dormitories was the beginning of my enlightenment regarding the possibilities of the future."

Her first teaching assignment was in Binghamton, N.Y. "I took the job simply because they offered it to me," she says. "I was a visiting art teacher for schools in the township. I didn't have a car, so I had to hitchhike and take the bus. Sometimes, I'd visit two schools in one day, and the head of the art department drove me back and forth."

Her next job was as an art teacher at Copiague Elementary Long Island. When she was 26, she got married to a Scandinavian extrovert from Minneapolis.

"My parents disapproved of interracial marriages," Susan says. "They told me that they would disown me, and they meant it. Whenever I telephoned my parents to make arrangements to visit them, they would say, 'We disowned you—hang up the phone.' My sister, Lynn, who was my maid of honor, was the only family member brave enough to attend my wedding."

Susan and her new husband moved to Chicago where he sold advertising space for a magazine. Susan found work as a second grade teacher with the Chicago school system.

"I taught for two years in Cabrini Green district, where Dr. Martin Luther King was assassinated," she recalls. "I have everlasting memories of April 4, 1968. I was teaching that morning, and I usually pulled down the shades to reduce the sun's glare. When I raised the shades again, I saw many police squad cars lined up in front of the school. When the teachers were notified what had happened, we were told to hold the children in class until lunch, and then let them go home. When the teachers left later, we had to drive through a large group of rioting high school students. It was a sad and violent day."

The couple lived in Chicago for two years, then moved back to Manhattan for her husband's new job at *Gourmet Magazine*. He also got involved in acting with a small theater group.

"I got involved with the group as a volunteer, because I knew how to sew," says Susan. "This is where I became smitten with the prospect of designing costumes for the theater. A director I met there was moving on to another theater for his next job, and asked me to join him. My first costume designs were for a play called, "The Chronicles," at the Chelsea Theater, which was one of the theaters located in the now Brooklyn Academy of Music. At that time, Robert Kaufman, the art director, offered me a grant from State of New York to earn a master's degree in theater design at Brooklyn College."

When her marriage ended, Susan was a single parent with a one-year-old son. She had no money and no support from her family. She lived as a nomad, staying with friends for six months.

"I wanted to work in Broadway theater, but for that, I needed to pass the United Scenic Artist Local 829 Union test which I did," Susan says. "On Broadway, the competition was keen, and I had to hustle with all my might with all my connections. It took about two years before my hard work began to pay off. I would say I had luck on my side in being in the right places at the right times."

In 1984, Susan learned that the costume designer had left the Late Night Show at NBC-TV. She got an opportunity to work at the show for one week.

"That week turned into 32 years of employment," says Susan. "Again, I was lucky to be in the right place at the right time! To have a steady paycheck in my profession is a coveted situation."

I asked Susan if she could recall any times when she felt discriminated against because she was a woman or Asian.

Yes," she says. "If anything, I felt discriminated for being a single parent. During the 1970s, I applied for a job as a costume shop supervisor and was told that because I had a child, I would not be reliable. As for being an Asian woman, there is a stereotype or social notion that Asian women are passive. I assure you—I was never passive in the workplace."

Susan was responsible for costuming all the dance and comedy skits, working with stars like Bill Murray, Bruce Willis and Nathan Lane. "They were my favorites," she says. "There were very few women who did the comedy skits on the show. Demi Moore did some, and I thought she was a great person. I had to dress her in a bikini with ten index cards attached to her suit for the Top Ten Skit. Each card had a number and a catchy saying in the back of card. She would take them off one by one and handed them to Dave."

In the last year of Late Show, the writers wrote an amusing piece where Susan and Meryl Streep played the owners of an acting school. "I only had one line with her, and I said my line perfectly, but Meryl had to do her lines two or three times," Susan says. "I learned later that she does this on purpose. Chris Pine, who was in the movie 'Into the Woods' with Meryl, said that he ran lines with her once and she flubbed and stumbled. It's her way of making others feel more comfortable around her because everyone is so intimidated in her presence."

When the Letterman Show ended in May, 2015, Susan changed her work status to "freelance." She finally feels free to take the jobs she wants, rather than needs. She helped her son, Zack, found a successful company called Urbana Greens, which grows greenhouse hydroponic local, pesticide-free and sustainable microgreens and bouquet baby greens. His clients are well known restaurants in the New York City area.

Susan's Final Thoughts

If you're an artistic soul just starting out professionally, and want to make a living doing your craft, you must learn early on to separate your pride of artistic achievement from doing the job from which you get a paycheck. Just work really hard, stay focused and hang in there passionately for your dream.

I loved working on the Late Show, and I'm very grateful for the incredible memories. Every day was an exciting experience of working with talented people to make the deadlines. But if I'd had my druthers, I would have been doing period films or fantasy adventure or science fiction shows—inventive things.

If you are going to try and make a living as an artist, realize, at least while you're paying your dues, that when you become successful in your field you will be an example to other artists to realize *their* dreams. I love being a mentor to young artists who are trying hard to make it and stay there.

Janet Killian
with Mandy (left), Carlos and Joey

104

Janet Killian

Don't look for handouts. You have to work for what you want.

Biography

Janet Killian is president and founder of Gemini Janitorial Services, a commercial cleaning services company based in Wilmington, Delaware. She grew the company carefully to more than $2 million in annual revenues, one team member and one client at a time.

In addition to providing janitorial services to business offices, the company also specializes in construction cleanup. A number of area contractors depend on the Gemini team to make sure their newly constructed office is ready to make a good first impression on the new occupants.

George & Lynch, a local construction firm, was Janet's first customer in 1984, and the Gemini team continues to clean their offices to this day. Long-term relationships with dedicated customers have helped the company grow.

Janet is an entrepreneur in the true sense of the word. No matter the daily challenges, her customers know they can count on her to deliver janitorial services with care and attention to detail.

Although she comes from humble beginnings (there were nine people in her family), Janet worked hard and appreciated every opportunity that came her way. Early on, she had the chance to purchase another cleaning business. She hired the best workers she could find, and the rest is history.

Janet attributes her success to the dedicated people on her team. She listens to her employees and gets to know them, their strengths and personalities. She is frequently out in clients' workplaces, training and giving a helping hand.

Gemini Janitorial Services is a WBENC-certified 100 percent woman---owned business. Janet is very active in the business community, recently serving as president of Wilmington Women in Business.

Janet's Story

Janet Killian made a powerful impression on me in 2014 when she accepted the Entrepreneurial Woman of the Year award from the New Castle County Chamber of Commerce.

Shyly, but with great dignity, Janet climbed the stairs to the podium and spread out before her the pages of her acceptance speech. The first words she uttered stunned to absolute silence the crowd of more than 500 fellow entrepreneurs and chamber of commerce members.

"Most of you don't know that I suffered from debilitating panic attacks for more than 18 years before I knew what was wrong with me," she said. A woman at my table gasped. Janet Killian? Outspoken, outgoing, joyful, successful Janet Killian? No way!

Her speech continued. "When I was very young," Janet said, "my father was diagnosed with schizophrenia, and he spent most of his life in mental institutions. I was sure these panic attacks, which began suddenly when I was 14, were signs I was losing my mind."

As she spoke, describing her dark journey through fear into the light of healing and hope, I was reminded once again that one should never judge a book by its cover. Everyone has a story, and Janet's ultimate, courageous triumph reminds us that, one, some stories are even more painful than your own, and two, that anything is possible when you have the will and determination.

Janet's father, Nathan DiMatteo, was the son of Italian immigrants who settled in Delaware. Her mother, Priscilla Maine, was from Massachusetts. A dietician, Priscilla met her husband while doing an internship at the Veteran's Administration in Elsmere, Delaware.

"My father had his own radio and television repair business, which he operated from the house," said Janet. "He wasn't around very often, and I remember asking my mom where he was. She told me he was in the hospital, and I left it at that. What she didn't tell me was that my father had a terrible mental illness, which was diagnosed as paranoid schizophrenia. I didn't understand what that meant. My mother took care of us during the day, and at night, she worked the 11 to seven shift at the Sherwood Diner on Market Street.

The News Journal wrote an article about her once. The headline read, "Priscilla goes to work while most people go to bed."'

The young mother got her children up early, sent them off to school, slept until the kids came home, fed them, put them to bed, and went to work again.

"She was very much a survivor," said Janet. "She did what she had to do. There was no Social Security money. Most of the food came from our garden. Meat was very rare at our house. My mother got very creative with surplus food we received. I didn't mind the cheese, butter and peanut butter, but the spam and whatever kind of canned meat they gave us wasn't very good. One night mom cooked liver and told us it was steak. Not liking it, I stayed away from mom's steak from then on. I think that's why I'm not much of a meat eater today."

Janet's first panic attack, at age 14, took her by complete surprise while traveling on a Greyhound bus to visit people in West Virginia. She couldn't breathe, her heart pounded, and the world swirled around her like some crazy carousel ride. She felt stark, unreasoning terror that shook her to the core. Nothing overt had caused it. It had just—happened, and it would continue to happen in worsening episodes over the next several years.

When Janet was 16, her parents divorced, and her mother moved herself and her four children into a one---bedroom apartment, which was all she could afford. Her older brothers and sister, old enough to be on their own, moved out, leaving Janet, her mother and three sisters to fend for themselves.

"My mother said that my father typically racked up a lot of bills during any time he had been released from the hospital, and she couldn't pay them," said Janet.

At the age of 15, she worked full time in the summer through a government program, and at 16 worked as a waitress at the Harvest House in the Concord Mall, but found herself living in a vicious, repeating cycle of psychological torment.

"I'd work for a few months, experience a debilitating panic attack, and quit the job," said Janet. "Shortly thereafter, I'd get another job, and then another panic attack, and quit again."

Janet married for the first time at age 17, and the relationship lasted a little more than four years. Shortly after her divorce, she married again, this time for a 10-year period. At that time she received her diploma through a home study course.

"The panic attacks increased in severity over the years to the point where I couldn't go to the grocery store, or drive, or many of the other outside activities most people take for granted," said Janet. "I remember going to the grocery store, filling my cart with food and while standing in line I had a panic attack. I ran out the store, leaving the cart in the line! Then one night, while watching TV at 2:00 a.m., I heard someone talking about a book called, 'Don't Panic.'"

The next day, Janet called the 9th Street bookstore to see if they had the book. They did. She forced herself into her car and pulled up in front of the store, parking crookedly (and illegally) right in front.

"Fifty dollars later, which was the cost of the book and the parking ticket, my life changed," Janet said. "The book became my bible, my step---by---step guide to sanity, and my journey out of the darkness began."

Janet found a support group and began working on herself in earnest. She followed the instructions in her new book to the letter.

"It's important to be aware of your negative thoughts, and not let them take control," Janet said. "I bought packets of little, yellow round stickers from the office supply store and stuck them in prominent places—my car's dashboard, on the kitchen sink, on my mirrors, and on the wall opposite my toilet. Seeing a sticker, I'd ask myself, 'What are you thinking now?' It helped me become conscious of what was going on inside my head and change the conversation."

Janet says the book, "Self Talk," was another revelation. "It said to record a tape filled with positive affirmations, so I did. I played it continuously, all day long, sometimes listening, sometimes not. One day, my stepdaughter borrowed my car, and when she came home, she asked me if I was crazy. What a loaded question! It was so ironic, and I still laugh about it. Funny, years later, she developed panic attacks and I was able to help her.

Her improvement was so remarkable that the Mental Health Association asked her if she would lead a support group of her own, which she did. Six months later, she divorced and met husband number three, and he was another, painful, eye-opening catalyst for personal change.

"Well," she said, without blushing, "the third one was the worst. He was narcissistic and controlling, but instead of this letting me down, I worked on myself harder than ever. I realized I was attracted to a particular type of man: energetic and charming in the beginning but cruel and abusive later. I habitually ignored all of the early red flags and danger signals that any 'normal' woman would have run away from. Basically, I married the same character three times."

When she and the worst of three broke up, Janet moved into a girlfriend's 198-square-foot apartment with her three dogs. She remembers lying down on her bed, crying, and going into a life and death battle with her soul.

"I was so stressed out I developed dysplasia [an early stage in the development of cancer] in my breast and uterus," she said. "But I couldn't—wouldn't—let these things get the better of me. Now I realize that I had to go through every single thing I went through to become the person I am now."

Janet's only solace during the tough times, the only activity she truly enjoyed because it calmed her, was cleaning. It was an important insight. She'd learned through her recovery that people who worked doing something they loved enjoyed greater satisfaction and fulfillment in their lives.

"I put an ad in the paper as a house cleaner," Janet said, "and within a very short period of time I had one or two customers a day. Then, a man called me and asked if I'd like to clean his building on Wednesday nights and Saturdays. I worked very hard for a long time, and it took a physical toll."

Janet developed tendonitis in her elbow, forcing her to stop cleaning houses. She didn't, however, want to give up her commercial cleaning clients. And then, sweet destiny delivered an opportunity right in her lap. It came in the form of a man called Gary Penrod, a man she had met years earlier during one of her numerous day jobs.

"People come into your life for the strangest reasons," Janet said. "Gary was the client of a business I did word processing work for. Guess what he did for a living? He owned a janitorial company, sold it, then went into the business of buying and selling janitorial companies. On his advice, I got a line of credit and bought the company that is now Gemini Janitorial Services. He has been my greatest mentor."

Naming the business after her astrological sign, Janet ran the business out of her home. She conducted interviews with new employees at a local hotel. The business grew slowly but steadily, first renting a tiny one-room office, then a larger space with two rooms, then to a large house (which she counts as a mistake), then to an office in New Castle with "way too much warehouse."

"Now we're at Ashley Place in Wilmington," she said, "and I love it because I am surrounded by people. People give me strength. And I love to be out and about. I get a little down if I'm alone too long."

When I asked Janet to describe her biggest accomplishment, she looked at me in amazement.

"Fred," she said, "I don't know what you're saying. If I'm at all successful in business, it's because of the people that I have working for me. I don't set rules—they set the rules for me, the people who work closest with me and whom I trust, and I support them."

Before I could open my mouth to ask another question, she stopped me. "Wait!" she said. "I just thought of something I'm proud of. I taught myself QuickBooks. I knew nothing about accounting or bookkeeping, but I got myself to understand that software. My accountant comes in quarterly to make sure I'm doing things right, but I understand it, I really do! But the biggest accomplishment was my understanding of panic attacks and how to overcome them and live a happy and productive life."

Did she ever experience gender discrimination?

"Oh, yes," she said. "I know what that's like. In the beginning of my business, I knew it was important to get out into the community and network. Thirty years ago, all I could find were men's groups. If there were women's networking groups, I couldn't find them. Now keep in mind, I didn't know anything about networking. All I knew was I wanted to focus on bringing in business.

"I joined a couple of organizations," she continued. "Both were very clannish and the members were mostly older men. That told me something. And, no one would do business with me, or even consider it. They preferred to do business with the people [the good ole guys] they'd done business with for years, and they certainly weren't going to do business with me if I hadn't been in business for very long. After time, I dropped my membership. It was a waste of my time."

Another anecdote about Janet's experience with gender discrimination involves a machine called an auto scrubber and a dishonest vendor.

"It's a big floor cleaning machine that you walk behind," said Janet. "I think it weights 500 pounds. I paid a lot of money for it. One night, while being used at a local community center, the machine broke. The vendor, with whom I was spending at least $10,000 a month, fixed the machine and brought it back. The machine broke again. There was a lot of going back and forth, but you know what I found out? He had switched machines on me! And, you know why? Because he figured that because I was a woman I would never have known about it unless I took the trouble to check the serial numbers, which I did. I never did business with him again."

Eventually, she met a woman named Jennifer Bagley, who told Janet about Wilmington Women in Business (WWB) and the National Association of Women in Construction (NAWIC). Janet considers both of those organizations as very valuable to her professionally. She's on the board of NAWIC, is a past president of WWB, and is a supporter of several non-profit organizations.

Janet's revenues last year were about $2 million. I asked her what advice she'd give to women who are starting businesses.

"My advice is, don't look for handouts," she said. "You have to work for what you want. You have to be passionate about it. You have to know that you may spend very long hours. But, you'll get there! And even though I've got arthritis in my back and shoulders from hard physical labor, I would do it all over again. I love this life, and I love my business."

Janet's Final Thoughts

I don't let fear control my life. For anyone who is thinking about starting a business, my advice to you is, be responsible for yourself. Love what you are doing. Be committed, persevere through the rough times and stay focused! Learn to trust others, mentor those who need help, get rid of negative people in your life, and don't let anyone get in the way of your goals.

Rita Landgraf

Rita Landgraf

"Whatever your dream is, be persistent, because you can reach that dream."

Biography

Rita Landgraf was sworn in as Secretary of the Delaware Department of Health and Social Services on Jan. 22, 2009. As Secretary, she leads the principal agency charged with keeping Delawareans healthy—ensuring that they get the health care they need—and providing children, families and seniors with the essential services on which they depend.

Rita oversees one of the largest departments in Delaware's government, with an annual budget of $2 billion. Under her leadership, DHSS has provided a broad range of services to help families weather the worst economic crisis since the Great Depression while helping coordinate the state's response to health care reform efforts and the needs of Delaware's seniors, a fast-growing population. She co-chairs the Governor's Commission on Building Access to Community-Based Services, chairs the Health Fund Advisory Council, and is a member of the Delaware Hispanic Commission's Health and Social Services Subcommittee, Delaware Health Care Commission, and Delaware Center for Health Innovation Board. In January of 2015, she was selected to serve on the U.S. Department of Labor's new advisory committee on Increasing Competitive Integrated Employment for Individuals with Disabilities.

Rita is a former executive director of the National Alliance on Mental Illness Delaware and of The Arc of Delaware, which advocates for people with intellectual and developmental disabilities. She is also a former president of AARP Delaware. She is a co-founder of SOAR (Survivors of Abuse in Recovery), which celebrated its 25th anniversary in 2016 and Delaware CarePlan, created in 1999 to establish a special needs pooled trust for individuals with disabilities.

Rita's Story

My interest in Rita as a candidate for "Pearls" was sparked when I saw her speak on health care issues at a Wilmington gathering of women entrepreneurs and community leaders. She is an articulate, thoughtful, approachable and kind person who holds a position of enormous responsibility.

I knew nothing of her background and had only a vague understanding of what the Delaware Department of Health and Social Services (DHSS) was about, except that it was one of the largest government agencies in the state. I wanted to interview Rita because she'd been appointed by the Governor at a relatively young age to run it.

Rita was born at St. Francis Hospital in Wilmington, Del., to Charles and Jeanne Horst Mariani. She has an older sister, Terry, who lives in Maryland.

Her father spent most of his career at DuPont, working in a variety of positions in the facilities area and then transitioned to accounting. He passed away five years ago at 82.

"My dad took early retirement, which was probably a mistake because it left him with nothing to do," says Rita. "I found him a job as a crossing guard for New Castle County, which fit him to a tee because he loved children. He was like the Pied Piper of our little neighborhood."

Rita's mother was a registered nurse who kept her license into her 70s. Rita describes her as a happy person who loves being a caregiver—and still going strong at 86.

"She didn't work while we were children," says Rita, "but she went back to work at Foulk Manor North in North Wilmington when I was in high school. She did private duty nursing for an elderly woman—she gravitated toward children and the elderly. She and I spent a few summers together at Camp Archmere; she as a nurse and me as a junior camp counselor."

Both parents loved music and dancing and they often performed at nursing homes.

"My father had a beautiful singing voice," recalls Rita. "Mom did, too. They were always going out, doing things. When my sister and I were little girls, he'd play the accordion and we'd dance."

Rita was shy as a child and didn't have the same musical talent as her parents. "They wanted me to play the clarinet, and I tried, but in high school, the band director asked me to twirl a baton instead," she says, with a laugh.

There were many pleasant and memorable moments growing up, but many were overshadowed by the incest of the man she thought was her paternal grandfather. She didn't learn until after her father's death that the man wasn't actually a blood relative.

Rita doesn't mind being honest about her past. In fact, she's been public about it. It taught her perseverance and resiliency, and because she survived the trauma, she can be more effective in helping survivors of abuse and recovery. Twenty-five years ago, Rita created a nonprofit organization called SOAR, or Survivors of Abuse in Recovery.

"Early on I avoided talking about the abuse because it recreated the trauma for me," she says. "But no more. I now know that healing and recovery are possible. I want people who are suffering in silence to be able to get that treatment, and if my story helps them, then that's the best thing of all."

Rita credits her recovery to former Miss America (1958) Marilyn Van Derbur, also a survivor of incest. "If it weren't for her, I wouldn't have sought treatment," says Rita. "She was on the cover of People magazine in 1993, a time when I was struggling. She made me realize that I wasn't alone. She referenced an organization in Fort Worth, Tex., and I went there to do some intensive trauma work. It set me on the path to recovery."

Upon her return, Rita created SOAR with Valerie Marek, the current executive director, and Dr. Steve DiJulio, who holds a Ph.D. in psychology.

"Much of the program is based on what I learned in Texas," she says, "It's intensive outpatient therapy. Our initial focus was on adults. There are a lot of wounded adults out there who've never resolved their childhood traumas. Later, SOAR expanded to treat children. The earlier people get into treatment, get that early intervention, the better they are from a health perspective."

Perhaps it was her mother's influence, but Rita was an emotional child—and natural caregiver. "When I give, I get so much back in return," she explains. "To some degree, it's even selfish because I'm giving to get."

At 12, Rita had an experience that caused her to realize that her future was going to be about helping others, especially people with disabilities. She told me her, "Mike on the red bike" story.

"Mike lived in the neighborhood next to ours," says Rita. "There were a bunch of us kids, all around the same age, who would hang out, and Mike would ride his bike over and try to make friends. We made fun of Mike. He had an intellectual disability. I always knew in my heart that it was wrong to do that, and yet, I didn't do anything to stop it.

"One day, as Mike was leaving, I saw a tear running down his cheek," she continues, "and I remember thinking, *we wounded his soul*. And my soul felt wounded. In that moment I decided that I was going to specialize in helping people with disabilities. The stars fell into alignment to make that happen. Mike was one of my greatest early teachers."

In 1999, Rita created Delaware CarePlan, a nonprofit that creates special needs trusts for people with disabilities and for families with modest incomes. Her ambition was surprising, since her father, having been raised in a traditional Italian family expected Rita and her sister to lead respectable lives as homemakers.

"Dad was proud that my sister and I went to college," she says, "but he didn't believe that women should have careers. He thought it was okay for them to have jobs early, but only until they got married and had children. I can remember him saying, 'You're not going to be one of those career women, are you?' It's fun to watch my mom blossoming now at 86. She had always let my father rule the roost."

At the University of Delaware, Rita majored in Community and Family Studies. She worked as a receptionist at a health spa, and during summers, took care of a little girl named Crissy, who had severe cerebral palsy.

"I learned how to communicate with her without words because she couldn't talk," says Rita. "We created ways in which she could tell me when she liked something or when she didn't through her smile. If she especially didn't like something, she stuck out her tongue."

When she graduated, Rita did an internship with a United Cerebral Palsy program. She also worked with a program called the Client Assistance Program, which helps people who have conflicts or issues with the state's Department of Labor Vocational Rehabilitation program. Both experiences carried over into her work with the DHSS.

Rita has had a few mentors, but she puts a woman named Kathy Matt, the dean of the College of Health Sciences at the University of Delaware, on the top of her list. "She's a true innovator," Rita says. "She's putting UD on the map with its research and physical therapy program for patients with Parkinson's disease. She's great. We have set up a memorandum of understanding between my DHSS and UD so we can advance things together."

Rita met her husband, Kurt Landgraf, 20 years ago when he was CEO of DuPont Merck, a DuPont pharmaceutical company. At the time, she was executive director of The Arc, an organization that serves people with intellectual and developmental disabilities.

"He was in the audience at a presentation I gave," says Rita, "and afterward, he approached me and said, 'I like what you do, and I would like to adopt your organization.' Kurt has three sons, and his oldest, Christopher, has an intellectual disability. I credit Christopher as being the catalyst for Kurt and me to have had a relationship that led to marriage."

Before Governor Markell appointed Rita to her position as DHSS Secretary, she was president of AARP—the youngest president the organization ever had.

"I got to travel the state and talk to seniors," she says. "What they told me was that they wanted to age in place with dignity, with health care support people coming to them. They didn't want to live in assisted living facilities until they had to.

"In Delaware at the time, we didn't have many community-based programs that would support people in their homes," she continues. Since I've been secretary, we've been converting to community-based support. For every one person served in a facility, three people can be served in the community. It makes more sense from an economic perspective, and it's what the market has been asking for."

I asked her how she'd been "discovered" by the Governor and invited to assume the top post at the state's largest department.

"I'd known him for some time," Rita says. "I get to know a lot of people through my work with people with disabilities. He was one of my mentors. He taught me how to influence the legislative branch and the cabinet. But the person who is really responsible for my appointment is Scott Green."

Scott, an attorney, is president of the board of trustees at Delaware Technical Community College and executive director of the Delaware River and Bay Authority. When Rita met him, Scott was executive vice president at MBNA, which was an active partner for people with disabilities.

"I placed a lot of people at MBNA, so Scott and I became affiliated through that," explains Rita. "When Governor Markell was elected, Scott encouraged him to consider me for the position."

Rita describes her leadership style as participatory. "I like to empower my team," Rita says. "There are 11 divisions at DHSS, and each has a director and deputy. I also have executive directors running certain areas, such as my health care commission and financial empowerment office. So there are 35 leaders at DHSS. I tell them, 'You lead the entire department—you just happen to be overseeing one of our divisions.' In actuality, no one oversees just one area. We all cross over many divisional boundaries."

With 4,000 employees, the DHSS serves the elderly and people with disabilities, many who live in poverty. They also provide trauma-informed care.

"If people are coming through my doors, they're carrying a whole lot of trauma on their backs," says Rita. "How we approach them can either break their spirit or empower them. We try to cascade the continuum of care throughout our organization."

"This has been the greatest honor of my life, to be able to serve in the public sector," she says. "I embrace the department's mission, which is to advance and promote good health and well-being, to enhance self--- sufficiency, and to protect vulnerable populations."

Rita says she has problems with work/life balance and sometimes wonders if she's a workaholic. It just doesn't *feel* like work.

"I work harder in this position than I ever have before," she says. "It feels like I'm working 24/7. It's fun. It's who I am."

She's exaggerating. Rita does have a life. She likes to read and she and her husband own a house in Lewes. "I like spending time there, sitting in the sun, riding my bike," she says. "That's our getaway."

This is Rita's last year as DHSS Secretary because it's the end of Governor Markell's term in office. "There are many exciting things in my future," Rita says, "but my passion for people with disabilities won't change. I've learned a lot over the past eight years, and I really enjoy public and population health. I've been looking at the social determinants of health, and we're also engaged in the impact of gun violence from a health perspective. Then there's a huge addiction epidemic to deal with. There are many places I can land when my term is up."

Rita's faith has enabled her to survive and overcome life's trauma and disappointments. She witnesses people's pain and sorrow regularly.

"Whenever a hardship came along, I'd pause and remind myself that I wasn't in control—I can be a control freak sometimes," she says. "I remind myself that something else is intended for me. I must let go. It gets easier as I get older. There are miracles all around us, but we have to be open to them. We see the worst of mankind during a tragedy, but we also see the best of mankind. In the work I do, I see a miracle every day. I get to witness greatness. But you have to be open to it. Sometimes, I think we forget that."

Rita's Final Thoughts

Whatever your dream is, be persistent, because you can reach that dream. Sometimes you've got to modify it along the way, and then, sometimes, you're surprised because you're pulled a different way, and that different thing turns out to have been your real dream all along.

Set your aspirations high and keep working toward them. You get so much back in return when you do that.

Carla Markell & Rue

Carla Markell

"If you want to grow, you have to do something you haven't done before."

Biography

Carla Markell became the First Lady of Delaware when her husband, Gov. Jack Markell, was sworn into office on January 20, 2009. As First Lady, Carla has focused on at-risk children and volunteerism. A mentor to several youth since 2000, she personally has seen how the commitment of a caring adult can make a real difference in their lives. She believes that mentoring as well as an exposure to arts and sports can transform their lives.

Carla is a native of Newark, Del., where she and the future governor were classmates at Newark High School. She graduated from the University of Delaware with a major in human resources and early childhood education, and then worked primarily in corporate training and human resources. As First Lady, she has spent much of her time visiting agencies and companies throughout Delaware to meet with staff, nonprofit volunteers and community members.

Carla helps to champion a week of service each April, which joins Delawareans from the Governor's Commission on Community and Volunteer Service, the State Office of Volunteerism and members of the community. Since assuming the role of First Lady, she has worked with the Friends of Woodburn, Delaware Public Archives, and Winterthur Museum and Gardens in the ongoing process of renovating Woodburn, the governor's state residence, all of which has been done with the help of private donations and extensive volunteer efforts. The Markells have been married since 1990 and have two adult children, Molly and Michael. They have a dog, Rue, a mixed---breed.

Carla's Story

I was invited to a small, intimate dinner party at the home of an acquaintance, a philanthropist and staunch supporter of the Delaware arts community. To my delight, I was seated next to Carla Markell, whom I'd met before but hadn't really had the chance to become acquainted with on a deeper level.

I don't know how politically correct it is to admit this, but for the next couple of hours, I laughed my head off. Carla is funny, direct and down-to-earth. But what made an even bigger impression on me was that she was able to improve on nearly every *bon mot* I threw her way. At the risk of seeming immodest, I can joke with the best of them, but seldom is anyone able to out-quip me. Carla was with me every step of the way, often a step or two ahead, and if this had been a contest, she would have won.

Carla has integrity, and she's kind. She champions many causes and does what she says she's going to do. She shows up. She rolls up her sleeves. She speaks the truth. When I asked her to write the foreword to my first book about remarkable women—you're reading the second book—she obliged, and then actually did it.

Why do I bring that up? Because I think that you, dear reader, like me, have asked people we know to write referrals or endorsements for us, and they say, "Yes, of course!" and then you never hear from them again. Carla is a woman of her word, and I'm delighted to be able to share her story.

She was born at the Delaware Memorial Hospital in Wilmington, Del. Of course, she would not have known then that a man named Jack Markell, her future husband, had been born exactly one month earlier and was cared for by the same pediatrician, Dr. Levitsky. But then again, the Jack and Carla story is full of coincidences.

Her parents, Donald Lee and Joan Smathers, were erudite, intelligent and lovers of arts and culture. They met when they were both ushers at a Los Angeles theater.

"My father had a Ph.D. in organic chemistry and was also a pianist," Carla says "He went to Caltech and UCLA, studying with the finest chemists in the world."

Even though Carla's mother, Joan, was raised in Toronto, Canada, by parents who taught her fine manners and good diction,

Carla describes her mother's childhood as traumatic. Joan's father died when Joan was seven, and a year later, she suffered a yearlong bout with rheumatic fever. There were several stepfathers. The first two died; the third was unkind. During this third marriage, the family moved to Los Angeles, where Joan finished high school at night while working during the day.

"My mother delayed her own education while she put my father through school," says Carla. "That's just how it was back then. In 1952, after dad got his Ph.D., he was recruited to work at DuPont's Experimental Station and my parents moved to Delaware. They had two children—my older brother Scott, who's very smart and talented and whom I still see regularly, and me. My father left us when we were little."

Carla believes that her mother was genetically predisposed to depression. Both of Carla's parents were alcoholics, and when her father left, her mother increased her alcohol consumption and became addicted to prescription drugs.

When Carla was elected First Lady, she thought it would be important to others to share her story, and her mother agreed. Carla says, "Our home life was chaotic: it lacked structure and discipline, so my brother and I grew up with no boundaries. We were largely unattended. I wasn't a good student. We didn't have study habits, healthy food to eat or nice, clean clothes in the closet. I remember rooting through piles of undone laundry to find something to wear."

Over the years, Carla, while still a child, became her mother's mother, taking on grown-up responsibilities.

"I got jobs. I bought my own clothes and food," says Carla. "I negotiated with the car dealer to get a better bargain, and made sure the rent was paid. I did the laundry, cleaned the house and took care of the dog."

To fully illustrate what her childhood was like, Carla tells the story of a weekend trip to New York when she was 12 and her brother was 14. "First, understand that, deep down, my mother is a romantic, and deeply, perhaps excessively, compassionate," she says. "She feels the weight of the suffering of others, and back then, when she was still drinking, this emotional weight became debilitating at times.

"We stayed at the Chelsea Hotel, which was famous as a place where starving artists lived. My mother chose this as an opportunity to take on the suffering of these artists and to wallow in depression. Unattended, my brother and I got on a train and rode all the way to Harlem, considered at the time to be an extremely dangerous neighborhood. Another time, while looking out from our hotel room window on 23rd Street, we heard a loud bang, and someone across the street fell to the ground. It scared us to death!"

The next day, Carla's mother complained of a terrible headache, so they all went to Bellevue Hospital and sat in the emergency room for hours, watching shooting victims get rushed in for immediate attention. Having seen someone get shot the day before, the kids were understandably traumatized.

"A month later, my mother had a nervous breakdown," Carla continues, "and my brother and I went to live with my father. After a couple of years, life with my father became unpredictable, and I chose to move back with my mother. That's when I declared that I wanted a better life for myself than what my parents had, and I began to take charge of my life and make healthy choices."

Carla chose friends who did well in school or athletes who possessed self-discipline and determination. She'd survived enough unstable, self-destructive people.

"When I was a senior in high school, a friend of my mother's told me about Al-Anon," says Carla. "She saved my life. She saw that I was suffering, and rather than hold back and mind her own business, she stepped in and showed me that I didn't have to be a victim of the abuse going on at home. Through Al-Anon, I learned how to manage my family situation.

"It's a program that supports family members of alcoholics. They taught me I could not fix or cure my mother, and that it wasn't my fault," Carla adds. "They explained that alcoholism is a genetic disease, and that as a child of addicts I had a higher chance of becoming one, or marrying someone with the disease. They taught me to make healthy choices in relationships."

"It's important to observe how someone interacts with other people and their families," adds Carla. "It gives you insight into their true character."

By the end of her senior year, Carla's mother got sober and began her own recovery process. Carla's relationship with her mother got better in many ways, and she felt she was able to more fully share her feelings. She remembers a particular piece of advice her mother gave her: *It's better to stay single than to be married to someone who will mistreat you for the rest of your life.* Carla took this to heart.

The speaker at Carla's high school graduation was her classmate Jack Markell who'd been studying abroad his entire senior year. The school invited him to speak to his class and share what he'd learned. His speech was called, "You Don't Know How Lucky You Are," in which he shared what he had seen in impoverished areas of the world, such as India.

"I had known Jack for a while," Carla says. "We had worked together at Friendly's Ice Cream in Newark. He seemed stable, kind and *normal*. He had such a nice maturity about him. My mother later said to me, 'Who was that young man? He was so impressive! He's really got a lot going for him. That's the kind of guy you should marry, Carla.' I didn't see Jack again for 10 years, but during that time, when I dated various boys who perhaps didn't treat me as well as I deserved, my mother would say of each, 'He's a very nice young man, Carla, but he's no Jack Markell.'"

Carla knew she wanted a better life, but she was unsure what she'd be when she grew up. She loved animals, but didn't think she had the grades to get into veterinary school. So she earned her bachelor's degree with a double major in human resources and early childhood education.

"I've always loved kids and I was always drawn to helping vulnerable citizens," Carla says. "So I thought training to be a teacher was a good choice. But as it turns out, I didn't enjoy being in a classroom every day and sticking to the same routine. I like variety, new situations, experiencing all walks of life, and not necessarily knowing what's next."

Carla continued to teach while working as a waitress to make ends meet and figuring out her next move. As she pondered various options, she happened upon the book, "What Color is Your Parachute?" It was full of great advice.

"The book suggested that rather than doing job interviews, I should do information meetings," Carla says. "So, instead of applying for jobs, I'd sit down and talk to people. I was lucky to have lots of contacts, many of whom were parents of the children I'd taught, so I reached out to them and said, 'Hey, I'm thinking about transitioning out of teaching and I'd love to pick your brain about what you think might be interesting for someone with my experience, skills and background.' It was a great way to do a job search."

One of the people she spoke with was a man who ran the rehabilitation center where her mother had gone for treatment. "He'd been looking for a community services representative and hired me on the spot," Carla recalls. "The job required a lot of public speaking, so I'd go into schools and businesses and conduct corporate training to teach supervisors and managers how to intervene and help employees who had problems with addiction. It was wonderful to be able to draw from my own painful experience with addiction and be able to bring that value to other people who were suffering. Because I understood it, I was able to talk about it with heart and soul and passion, and really make a difference."

Three years later, Carla and Jack crossed paths again while planning their 10-year high school reunion. Jack and Carla had always been fond of each other and started getting together as friends. In time, he officially asked her out. Carla liked him very much, but was cautious.

"Jack was always very curious about who I was as a person and what kinds of things mattered to me," Carla says. "But I told him he really shouldn't have anything to do with me. After all, my family was loaded with baggage. I didn't want him to have to deal with that, because I just knew there would be trouble down the line. And you know what he said? 'I love you for who you are. I believe in you, and I think you are a wonderful person.' What a gift that was for me!"

After marrying in 1990, the couple moved to northern New Jersey, where Carla found work in corporate training. "I helped people who had been downsized deal with crises," says Carla. "Again, my background helped. As a child of alcoholics, I had grown up dealing with crises every day, learning how to defuse tense situations and work through emotional situations using patience and logic, so I was able to assist people in dealing with the painful transitions by showing them how to develop good résumés and create solid job search strategies."

Later, in her role as Delaware's First Lady, her background came into play yet again. "I'm much more effective because of my personal experience," she says. She spends a great deal of time working with at-risk children and speaking at schools about addiction issues.

"Kids need to know that they have choices and can be empowered to fight for themselves," Carla says. "People need to know that if they see a child in trouble, that it's okay to step up and tell them there's help out there. Too many people don't have the courage to enter another family's dynamic, but they need to. It may be the best thing that's ever happened to that young person."

Another skill Carla learned from her childhood experience is the ability to set healthy boundaries. "I start with being good to myself," she says. "I get in my exercise almost every day and eat healthy foods. If I begin to feel like something is tasking me too much, I say no. I'm careful about not over-committing myself. This is especially helpful in politics. I like having the ability to help draw greater attention to certain causes and organizations. I want to help them all, but I can't. No one can. I've needed to put up boundaries. I learned a lot of these skills from the programs at Al-Anon.

"When Jack told me he was running for Governor, I was fearful but I knew that this was something he had in his heart and soul," says Carla. "So I stood beside him despite my fear, and told him that I would support him. When I was determining what my own role would be, I heard Michelle Obama speak, and she said that she'd been nervous, too. And she had a great strategy for stepping into the First Lady role and learning the ropes."

Carla followed Michelle Obama's lead by visiting various state agencies and thanking them for the work they were doing, and letting them know how much she appreciated them. It helped ease her into the job and overcome her fear.

"I was afraid of people's expectations," says Carla. "I didn't want to disappoint anyone. Our state workers are amazing, and they have the hardest jobs serving clientele in our prisons, psychiatric hospitals and the Division of Motor Vehicles. I have such gratitude in my heart for how hard they work, and it was such a pleasure to be able to personally thank many of them."

The first state agency Carla visited was Ferris School for Boys, an American Correctional Association-accredited treatment facility that provides services for up to 72 court-committed males, ages 13 to 18.

"I was blown away by the fact that it could be any of our kids in their situations, had they grown up under the same circumstances," Carla says. "If they'd had a more structured, healthy upbringing, their lives would have been better. I have a heart for those kids."

Carla and Jack have two children: Molly, born 1993, a University of Pennsylvania graduate who, at the time of this writing, was in New Zealand on a one-year working visa, and Michael, born 1995, who is a sophomore at Brown University studying computer science.

"You know what I'm doing tomorrow?" asks Carla. "I'm going to the Nobel Laureate Dinner at the Swedish Embassy and giving the closing speech. Who would have thought that Carla Smathers from Newark, Del., would be privileged enough to stand up before Nobel Prize winners? It's crazy, but I'm doing it. It's funny how life turns out when you've learned through hardship to make the right choices."

Carla's Final Thoughts

Every person has difficult situations that are very hard to overcome. But you've got to believe in yourself and have faith that good things are in store for you. You have to be willing to open your heart and allow things to happen. Don't let fear stop you. When I was in Al---Anon, I ran across a poem called "Risks," by Janet Rand. It inspired me. The final line is, "Only the person who risks is truly free." Take a risk and pick up that phone and do an information meeting. Take a risk to get yourself out of your comfort zone to try something new.

Be yourself. Learn to be comfortable in your own skin. Follow your inner voice, your intuition, and let it take you to the next level in life, whatever that is.

Kathy Matt

Kathy Matt

"Focus on the opportunities more than on the challenges, and be grateful for them. Opportunities beget opportunities."

Biography

Dr. Kathy Matt has served as the dean of the College of Health Sciences at the University of Delaware since 2009. During her time as dean, she has been instrumental in developing the Health Sciences Complex on the Science, Technology and Advanced Research (STAR) Campus, which was created on the site of a former Chrysler assembly plant.

The Health Sciences Complex integrates a primary care clinic that offers nutritional counseling, mental health services, fitness and exercise counseling, physical therapy speech language hearing clinics, and shared interdisciplinary and translational research labs—all of which are state of the art facilities for experiential learning and collaborative research.

The onsite Healthcare Theatre program is used to train health professions students in the art of medicine. The First Steps program funds undergraduate teams that take on health care challenges and design solutions. This new facility focuses on identifying biomedical challenges at the bedside, studying them in the lab, and then translating discoveries back to patients in ways that lead to better diagnostics and treatment plans.

The campus is created as a platform that facilitates collaboration across academia, business and the community. Dr. Matt also serves as the executive director of the Delaware Health Sciences Alliance (DHSA)—a 501(c)3 partnering Christiana Care Health System, Nemours/Alfred I. duPont Hospital for Children, Thomas Jefferson University and the University of Delaware—and co---director of UD's health education partnership with Thomas Jefferson University.

Kathy's Story

Dr. Kathy Matt sees Delaware as a microcosm of the nation, and she says its small size lends itself towards everyone working together to contribute knowledge, educate future health care professionals and conduct research that develops evidence-based medicine. That's a good thing. Kathy envisions Delaware as a future leading presence of the global medical community.

How do you form an impression of someone you've never met? In my experience, not so much by watching them in action, but by what others say about them. It's right about brands as it is about individuals. Word of mouth is one of the most important ways people and businesses establish good reputations. Kathy has built a strong personal brand that convinces people to have faith in her intelligence, leadership and capability before they've even met her. How? Great word of mouth.

If you're consuming this book alphabetically and have read the chapter about Rita Landgraf, who is, as of this writing, serving her last term as Secretary of the Delaware Department of Health and Social Services, you might recall that she called Kathy "a true innovator," and someone at the top of her mentor list. That's impressive.

Kathy was born at Sacred Heart Hospital in Chester, Pa., to Kathleen and Walter Matt, both native Pennsylvanians. She is the third of four children—all girls.

"I'm named after my mother, who was named after *her* mother," says Kathy. "At the time of my birth, my parents lived on North College Street in Newark. I was born in Chester because of my mother's attachment to where she had grown up, and the doctor she knew there. It was important to her that I be born at Sacred Heart."

Kathy's father was an eighth-grade science teacher who dreamed that all of his children would go to college. Concerned that he wouldn't be able to pay tuitions on his schoolteacher's salary, he moved his family to Newark so they could be close to the University of Delaware campus and establish residency.

"Dad taught in the Newark School District for more than 30 years," Kathy says. "He was also the football coach at Newark High School."

Kathy's mother was a stay-at-home mom with unlimited energy. "She did a million things and was a fabulous cook and an even better baker," says Kathy. "Mom loved a good celebration—birthdays, holidays—there was so much pride in everything she did."

Inspired by pleasant baking experiences seared into memory, Kathy began working at Newark icon Bing's Bakery when she was 16. It was her first job.

"I learned baking from the best," says Kathy. "I started as a cake finisher, and it took me a very long time to learn how to do it well. Mrs. Bing used to joke with me that if she paid me 25 cents for every cake I got done, I wouldn't be making very much money."

She worked at Bing's for years, all through her undergraduate years at University of Delaware (UD), and during the holiday rushes while she worked on her master's degree, also at UD. When Kathy stepped into her recent position as dean of the UD College of Health Sciences, she helped her daughter, Carolyn, get a job there.

"She called me on a busy holiday weekend—Easter, I think—and said, 'Mom! We're so busy! Can you come in and help?' I was happy to. Now, if you've ever been to Bing's, you know you can look directly back into the kitchen where the cake decorators are working. Gina, my chief of staff, came in with her family to buy pastries, and I heard her say, 'Oh, and there's my boss, right there.'"

Kathy's parents taught their four daughters that there were no limits to what they could achieve. If they worked hard enough, they could accomplish anything.

"My parents were very hard workers," Kathy says. "We grew up in a culture that appreciated self-sufficiency. If the TV broke, my father fixed it, and we girls helped. I can still remember trying to figure out how to get those little tubes out. If the car didn't work, he'd figure it out, and we pitched in. He wanted to impress upon us that we needed to take care of ourselves."

Kathy was a shy child. "My mother always says that I'm overcompensating for that now," she says. "I was quiet, but I worked very, very hard."

She fell in love with science at an early age and began to think about going to medical school.

"It's because of my dad," Kathy says. "Because he was an eighth-grade science teacher, we were always out catching frogs for his science class. We'd take long walks together, and he'd ask a gazillion questions about biology. I just loved that."

Kathy never thought she'd wind up in education. After having watched her father in action, teaching looked like too much hard work. When she was an undergraduate majoring in biology at UD, however, she became a lab assistant. That required her to do some teaching, and she loved it.

"A string of wonderful mentors guided me on a path I hadn't expected to take," she says. "In high school, teachers gave me a love of physiology, which prompted me to ask lots of questions, which prompted a UD professor to invite me to work in his lab, doing research. I cleaned cages and he did research work on animals. Then he invited me to help with a research project, which led me to get a master's in biology."

During her junior year, Kathy, who chose German for her foreign language requirement, applied for an Austrian-American scholarship to go to Austria.

"I spent the summer in Salzburg, studied German, and also took classes in music and art history," she says. "I fell in love with the mountains there."

To earn a Ph.D. in zoology and continue her animal research, Kathy went to the Seattle's University of Washington, which was considered one of the finest zoology departments in the country. It was during this time that she met her future husband Mike Moore.

"I knew a guy who would be perfect for my roommate, so I set up a blind date," she says. "A group of us met at a bar, and while we were drinking beer, my roommate left, and Mike and I became a couple instead. We got married after we'd both finished defending our dissertations."

Before they got together, both Mike and Kathy had applied for post-/doctoral funding at the National Institute of Health—and both requests were granted.

"The person Mike got funded to work with was at Harvard, and mine was at the University of Texas Health Science Center in San Antonio, where I wanted to look at molecular mechanisms by using animal research," Kathy says. "Luckily, Mike's person left Harvard to move to Austin. We moved to New Brownsville, Texas, which was right in the middle."

Following his post-doctoral studies, Mike accepted a professorship at Arizona State University in Tempe, Ariz. Kathy remained in Texas to finish her work then followed her advisor to Illinois to help set up his lab.

"It was a commuter marriage," Kathy explains. "When I finished my post-doc, I got a job at Northeastern Ohio College of Medicine. Mike and I got together whenever we could, and eventually decided that we didn't want to live apart."

Arizona State University (ASU) offered Kathy a visiting professorship plus start-up money. She took it, but she wasn't thrilled about it. For one thing, it wasn't a tenure-track position. For another, she felt a bit of gender bias. If her husband were a professor, people would ask why she wasn't satisfied. What more could she possibly want? Then there was the Arizona climate.

"I'm not a desert person," she says. "It's hot and sandy, and I like four seasons. Mike loved it. As an ecologist and field biologist, living in the desert allowed him to look at changes, hormones and behavior in lizards."

Kathy says that she and her husband are opposites, in terms of personality. He's low-key, whereas she's talkative and animated. Not many of their co-workers and students at ASU realized they were even married. They preferred to keep their private life private.

"One day, a student came running into my office," she recalls, "saying, 'Oh my gosh, I heard the most amazing rumor today. It's hilarious—you'll die!' 'What was it?' I asked. 'Somebody said that you and Dr. Moore are married, like *that* could ever happen!'"

Eventually Kathy did get a tenure-track job in the kinesiology department, researching athletic amenorrhea, a condition that affects female athletes when strenuous training halts menstrual cycles. She was at ASU for 20 years, starting as an assistant, then associate and finally, full professor.

"I had some amazing experiences there," says Kathy. "One of them was doing a Congressional Fellowship, which was a life changing experience. The Endocrine Society and the American Association sponsored me for science. For a year I had an office in Washington, D.C., where I worked for Senator Jeffords, who chaired the Health, Education, Labor and Pension Committees. It gave me an opportunity to see how research translates into policy."

When she returned to Phoenix, having worked with Jeffords, who happened to be friends with ASU's former president, Lattie Coor, Kathy's status soared, rendering more high---profile opportunities. One of them was when then-governor Janet Napolitano called university presidents together and said, "We're going to have a medical school in Phoenix, so figure it out!"

"The new president of ASU, Michael Crow, reached out to me, and I became one of the founding faculty of the University of Arizona/ASU Medical School in downtown Phoenix. It was a major coup, and a wonderful experience—U of A and ASU are fierce rivals, especially on the football field. Luckily, when I was in D.C., I learned valuable skills, the most important of which was that it's the meetings before the meetings and all of the details underneath that make things happen. Things can totally unravel like a ball of yarn and you don't even see it coming. I love all of that."

Another rule to live by, says Kathy, is that a "yes" is a "yes," and "no" is "maybe." She learned that from another mentor, Jim O'Brien, who was Michael Crow's chief of staff.

"I got to know him while ASU developed a partnership for education and research with the Mayo Clinic, which had a hospital in Scottsdale," Kathy says. "One day Jim said to me, 'If there's something you're trying to do, and you get a 'no,' you asked the wrong person.'"

One day, quite unexpectedly, Kathy got a note that UD President Pat Harker was making a stop in Phoenix as part of his regular tour of the country.

"I hadn't been in touch with UD for years," she says, "so I attended his presentation at the Wrigley Mansion. He was very charismatic, and his vision for UD was exciting. Someone asked him if he planned to start a medical school, and he answered that they were forming the Delaware Health Science Alliance, which was all about partnerships."

Kathy introduced herself and talked about her work with partnerships at ASU. Afterward, as she waited for the valet to bring her car, she noticed Harker leaving the building, and took a bold step.

"I don't know what made me do it, because the shy me wouldn't have," she says. "I was carrying several folders about biomedical partnerships and all the things we were doing at ASU and the strategies we used. I pulled out one of the folders, went up to him and said, 'President Harker, these are the things we're doing in biomedical partnerships. I'm just wondering if there's anything I can do to help?"

Months later, UD announced that a dean's position was opening up and she applied, just for the fun of it. Provost Dan Ridge interviewed her, but she didn't have to talk much. Harker had already provided him with everything he needed to make a decision. But the interview process wasn't over. The next step was to meet with all the vice presidents, and they had tough reputations.

"The vice president of IT was the first to speak," says Kathy. "He said, 'I have a question first that I want to ask before we get to the others. Was your dad an eighth-grade science teacher?' and I said, 'Did your sister teach at Glasgow?' I was in!

"I feel like Arizona was fabulous," she continues, "but in retrospect, I was practicing for UD. My dad was a brilliant man, and he chose to raise his family in Newark. I feel like I have a lot to thank the community for. I wanted to come back and give back."

Kathy doesn't talk much about gender discrimination. She believes that if women felt encouraged, they'd also feel empowered to cry foul when facing discrimination.

"Women tend to undervalue and undersell what they do," she says. "They need to learn how to put themselves in the best light, and to know the rules of engagement."

Kathy has a couple of stories about women whose careers were thrown off track by discriminatory practices.

"My husband and I had the same advisor during our doctoral programs," she says. "When we got engaged, I thought telling our advisor was the right thing to do. Later, at a dinner party, my advisor's wife said, 'I heard the news that you're getting married. What will you do now?' The question puzzled me. 'I'm going to do my post-doc,' I said. 'Oh,' she said, 'I didn't expect that you were going to continue.' I learned later that years prior, she and her husband, both graduate students, had applied for fellowships, but since they were married, only one would be eligible for funding. She was dropped and never continued her studies.'"

Another woman, Kathy says, was a physician, but she'd wanted to be a veterinarian. Women weren't being accepted into veterinary school.

"When I was pregnant with my first daughter, Carolyn, professors had to work out with their department heads how much leave they could take," says Kathy. "There was no official policy for how much leave a professor could take. I was out for one week and brought a playpen to the office. It was only a problem when students came in to complain about their grades and the baby was crying."

Carolyn is now a sociologist at UD. Kathy's other daughter, Kelly, is an English major at Skidmore College in upstate New York.

The truth is, we've only scratched the surface of who Kathy Matt is. Adequately describing her life, her many achievements, disappointments and challenges would take many more pages.

But she does love to bake, and so I think her leadership genius can be compared to baking. She puts together all the right ingredients, stirs them up, puts them into a partnership of strong---minded individuals, watches them rise, pulls the finished product of the oven, then lets it cool. With Kathy at the helm, everything else that happens is just icing on the cake.

Kathy's Final Thoughts

There are no wrong answers, and there are no wrong decisions. You make a decision, believing it to be the best one. You totally have the capacity to do that. By not making a decision, you're making a decision. Unfortunately, not enough people realize that. I know I'm probably wrong sometimes in what I do or what I choose, but I think it's very important to be proactive and make the decision.

You make partnerships work on two levels. It's a sandwich. You've got to work at the highest level and then the lowest. You've got to get the buy-in. At the same time, if things aren't working, you've got to jump back up to the top and say, 'okay, this isn't working and here's why.' You and the leadership team need to tell people what needs to happen.

I think there's real value in believing the sky's the limit. You've got to figure out where you want to go. I tell my students that there's not a straight line from A to B. It's a circuitous route.

Every experience you have becomes a part of you. It allows the next thing to happen, even if it seems unrelated. Sometimes you think things are getting off track, but they're actually not. Life is a circle, and it's winding, and every little piece adds to it. Be open to all opportunities, and that involves listening to people. Focus on the opportunities more than on the challenges, and be grateful for them. Opportunities beget opportunities.

Alisa Morkides

Alisa Morkides

"Whatever you want to do, do it well. Be good at it. Be an expert. Be obsessed with it."

Biography

Alisa Morkides is the founder and owner of Brew Ha Ha!, an independent chain of coffee houses headquartered in Wilmington, Delaware.

Alisa started her career as a bench chemist, working for the Upjohn Company in Kalamazoo, Michigan. After a year of toiling in the lab—and accidentally setting her lab hood on fire on occasion—she realized that a behind-the-scenes role as a scientist wasn't her passion.

She went back to school, earned an MBA, and held management positions with several large Philadelphia-area corporations. After a decade of moving from one tedious job to another, learning to dread Mondays and love Fridays, she finally learned that big business wasn't for her. She left the corporate world with the goal of pursuing a long-held dream to start her own business.

A vacation to Florence in the spring of 1993 changed everything. She fell in love with the quality coffee experience in Italy. One day, while sitting on a rose-covered terrace overlooking Florence, sipping yet another perfect cappuccino, she thought to herself, "Why can't they make coffee like this in Wilmington?' And then she thought, "Wait a minute, why can't I make coffee like this in Wilmington?" And a seed was planted.

When she got back from vacation, she pushed full steam ahead into opening Wilmington's first bona fide espresso café. She opened her first Brew Ha Ha! café in December 1993—in the middle of a recession and a brutally cold winter. Business was slow, cash was tight, but the few customers that were able to brave the snow and ice loved the coffee and the concept.

In 2015, Alisa opened a second business, Brandywine Coffee Roasters, which is on track to roasting and selling 70,000 pounds of coffee in its first full year of operation.

Alisa's Story

The coffee house, or café, has been around since before the 17th century as a gathering place for people to socialize, write, exchange ideas and sip endless cups of coffee. They're a relatively new phenomenon in the United States, but we've come to think of them as pleasant sanctuaries for people to discuss business, read books or simply hang out and reflect with their favorite coffee drink.

The best coffee houses, in my opinion, are the ones that feel like home, with big, overstuffed chairs, eclectic furnishings, a fireplace, perhaps bookshelves and a pleasant patio in front or out back. I like cozy.

When I googled "coffee house," Alisa Morkides's Brew Ha Ha! came up at the top of the list. That she's there by virtue of intelligent search engine optimization doesn't matter, because, in my opinion, the top of the list is where she ought to be. In all of her locations, she's created an atmosphere that fairly hugs you with flavor and taste, as much with the coffee as with ambience.

Alisa was born in Birmingham, Alabama to Mona and Stanley Lippincott. Her brother, Steven, was born 13 months later. She calls him her "Irish twin."

Her mother, a native Alabaman, was born into a poor family in the small town of Jasper, reached by long, winding unpaved roads.

"My mom grew up on top of a hill of red dirt," says Alisa. "The grass didn't grow there. She lived in a simple, wood frame house with an outhouse in the back."

Mona's family were strict Baptists, and though economically challenged, they were smart and ambitious. Alisa says they were rocket scientists—literally.

"My grandfather had to quit school when he was 14 and go to work in the mines," Alisa says. "Later, he started his own business repairing mine equipment. He was a brilliant man. One of my uncles, a nuclear physicist, worked in the space program at NASA. The other uncle graduated from high school at the age of 14 and became an actuary. He, too, worked in the space program at NASA."

Mona, also brilliant, aced her way through high school and became the State of Alabama's debating champion. But her family, despite its wealth of intelligence, was victim to the Great Depression, and their region of the country was hit especially hard. It took decades to recover.

Like her mother before her, Mona was expected to stay home, raise kids and be a homemaker. She married Alisa's father, Stanley, at the "ancient" age of 23 (most girls married at 18), after a brief, two-- month courtship. She postponed her college education until Alisa and her brother were in high school, earning a degree in Spanish with a minor in math.

Stanley, who hailed from Pennsville, N.J., was a DuPont executive who'd been transferred to the company's Birmingham plant. He met Mona and proposed two months later. Alisa came along, and then Steven.

"After a couple of years, my dad was transferred to Maryland, then Minnesota, then Wilmington, then Brazil. Ultimately, we ended up back in Wilmington, which was my dad's home turf."

Stanley's family was from the old, Quaker Lippincott family line. Though they weren't practicing Quakers, they preserved the Quaker temperament of conservatism, thrift and steadiness.

"They were the opposite of my mother's family," Alisa says, "who were vivacious and argumentative, whereas my father's family was sober and reliable."

Her father's grandfather was a house painter who worked for DuPont for 30 years painting equipment at the plant, and Stanley followed in his footsteps with his three decades at the company.

Mona and Stanley divorced when Alisa was 28. She says it was a tumultuous marriage, perhaps because of the brief courtship and that the two were entirely different. But as difficult as the marriage was, Mona remained strong for her children.

"She is a driven person," explains Alisa. "I think her uniqueness is her unwavering commitment to education and to doing what was necessary. She did a great job. She was a strong woman who could do what she wanted, and she was a role model for me."

After earning her college degree, Alisa's mother became one of the top Realtors in Wilmington for more than 20 years.

"Essentially, when you're a real estate agent, you have your own business," says Alisa. "You need to decide how successful you're going to be because you're in sales. Mom was good at that. She was a perfectionist, and tough at times, but I attribute much of my business success to her."

Although outgoing and gregarious as a young child, suddenly, in middle school, Alisa's spirit went within and she became what some of her close friends call, "pathologically shy."

"Perhaps it's because we moved around a lot," she says. "It wasn't easy for me to make new friends. I was uncomfortable and felt that I didn't fit in. After a while, it was overwhelming, and I'd skip school to go ice skating."

When she was in eighth grade, Alisa avoided school nearly altogether and spent her time at the ice rink. By the end of the semester, many big school assignments were due, which she hadn't even started. Lucky for her, her father was transferred.

"I can't believe I got away with it!" says Alisa. "My cover would have been blown. My parents never knew about the ice rink, and they'd never seen any of my report cards."

After the transfer, Alisa wound up at Springer Junior High School. She says she sat by herself at lunch every single day for a year and a half.

"It was a big class—like 500 people—and I didn't have any friends," says Alisa. "I didn't know how to make them. I didn't go to my prom, either. I wouldn't say that was devastating to me, not to go. I never thought I'd be asked, to be frank, and I wasn't. What's sad to me, looking back, is how little self---esteem I had at the time."

Alisa got her first taste of being an entrepreneur when she was 15. "I set up a guitar instruction school in my house," she explains. "I played classical guitar. I taught myself to play when I was 11, practicing so hard my fingers bled. I'd walk up to Lanning Music on Concord Pike every day and buy sheet music from all different kinds of artists: Andre Segovia, Doc Watson, whoever. I was really into Spanish guitar."

She decided she would earn extra money teaching guitar, so she found a little typewriter, painstakingly created 500 announcements and stuffed them into all of the neighborhood mailboxes.

"No one called me because the announcements were cheesy looking," says Alisa, "but the guy at Lanning Music was kind enough to put me on his referral list, and it wasn't long before I had 15-20 students from the local high school. Sometimes the students improved so quickly I was only a little bit better than they were."

It was a given in Alisa's family that she would go to college. It was assumed that she'd meet a man in college, get married, maybe work for a few years, and then have children, which she would raise while supporting her husband in his career.

"I remember feeling pressured about my weight," she recalls. "After all, if I was going to meet Mr. Right in college, I needed to look good. And in the 1970s, that meant being very skinny. Today, I'm right in the ballpark, but back then, I might have been 10 to 15 pounds higher than skinny. That drove my family crazy."

Alisa had always wanted to be a writer, but she was told that majoring in English was not a practical thing to do.

"I majored in chemistry because my father had majored in chemistry," Alisa says. "Also, my rocket scientist uncles were big with science, and I wanted to please them, and make them think that I was smart. I always had the feeling that I wasn't as smart as the other people in my family. My parents paid my college tuition, luckily, but they may not have if I'd majored in English."

At Bucknell University, Alisa became a party animal, losing her shyness after sipping grain alcohol out of giant trashcans.

"Bucknell was a great school, and I'd worked really hard to get in, but in those first two years I nearly flunked out," Alisa says. "In my third year, I decided to get my act together and actually made the Dean's list."

Graduating with a bachelor's in chemistry, Alisa went to work for the Upjohn Company in Kalamazoo, Mich. as a bench chemist, doing quality control tests on the night shift from 3 p.m. to midnight.

"I hated it," she says. "I had no social life at all and had to wear a shapeless white lab coat. One night, in my haste, I accidentally set my lab hood on fire. My boss calmly put the fire out, and wrote in my personnel file, 'needs improvement.' I decided to get out of Kalamazoo, where it snows at least 1,000 inches a year. I might be exaggerating, but not by much."

Alisa went back to school at the University of North Carolina and earned an MBA in finance.

"That's where I learned that 50 percent of my grade would be based on class participation," she says. "If you didn't participate, you flunked out, so even though it caused me many a sleepless night, I made myself speak in class—actually got up in front of people and talked. I got through it."

While studying business, Alisa got back in touch with that part of herself that had always yearned to be an entrepreneur. "The concept of entrepreneurship was very much at odds with what was going on in Wilmington at the time," says Alisa. "In Wilmington, it was all about working for the 'man,' who was DuPont, if you were a man. If you were a woman, you worked for somebody until you found a man to marry. But the key thing was, you didn't start your own thing. It was one thing for me to have a guitar school or a little catering company that lost money, but to actively start a grown---up business was actively discouraged by family, friends and society at large. But in business school, I got a really good grade in my entrepreneurship class."

For her class assignment, Alisa found a beautiful, old Victorian building and proposed turning it into condominiums. She thought of taking on the project after graduation, but lost her nerve, telling herself she didn't have the money to make it work. Instead, she scored a job as a financial analyst at Rohm & Haas in Philadelphia, and afterward went to work at the Franklin Mint as a financial and marketing manager. Then, at the age of 31, she met her first husband and moved to Texas.

Throughout the next several years, Alisa tried her hand at different kinds of entrepreneurial ventures. One was an online business selling used cars. Her first husband was an IT expert who was able to help her set it up, but as she worked her way through the business plan, the idea lost its attraction.

"I love decorating, I liked making miniature furniture in half---inch or one-inch scale, and I loved the beautiful mini---mansions on display at the Chicago Museum," says Alisa. "I loved making the furniture, needle-pointing the rugs, electrifying the rooms and putting up the wallpaper. I wanted to make giant dollhouses and then sell them. I had a lot of passion for it, but no talent. My furniture wouldn't stay glued together, and the little tables and chairs fell apart in my hands. Worse, there was no money in it. I tried for a year, but it just didn't work out."

Alisa next decided she wanted to be a certified financial planner. She earned her CFP and set up a broker-dealer relationship with a company in Lancaster, but she backed out of it. She found herself incredibly bored with the whole idea.

"It took me a couple of years to earn the CFP, but suddenly, I couldn't imagine myself doing that kind of work," Alisa says. "I don't care about changing tax codes. But there I was again, trying to figure out what I was going to do next. I'd tried and tried to create my own businesses, but nothing had worked. My then husband invited me to be an accountant at his company. I thought, hmm, I could be the comptroller or even the CFO! Six months later, my husband's business partner fired me and put his wife, who had no accounting experience, in the position. I was devastated."

In 1992, Alisa and her husband traveled to Italy for vacation, and she fell in love. "Italy was amazing," she says. "I felt reborn—the culture, the architecture, the coffee shops—that's where I got the big idea. While everyone else went off to museums, I'd go to the local coffee shop, drink fantastic cappuccino and gaze at the rose-covered garden, the Duomo, the beautiful church in the distance, and the twinkling lights. What if, I thought, I could bring an experience like this back with me to Wilmington?"

When she returned to the States, she wrote the business plan immediately. "I had probably written five or six business plans by this point," Alisa says, "but this one practically wrote itself. Before I knew it, I had leased space in Greenville and opened my first café."

She didn't have any money. Her then husband, Mike, had a business, but it had dramatic ups and downs and wasn't a steady paycheck. "We had $17,000 in the bank, and Mike was understandably upset," she says. "He was disappointed I wasn't pursuing a career as a CFP after I'd worked so hard to get the certification. I told him not to worry; that I'd been told that the deepest we'd go financially was $10,000, so he, seeing how badly I wanted it, agreed."

Unfortunately, the $10,000 Alisa had been advised to expect turned into $60,000 after equipment and build-outs. She convinced the landlord to give her an interest---free loan, but she was still way over budget. But the real trouble had just begun.

"We opened the café on December 1, 1993," she says. "It was the beginning of a recession—a big one. And, it was a really cold, snowy winter. People couldn't get to the café unless they had four---wheel drive. We didn't make money in the first two years, but there was a special magic about it, and I knew it was going to work. Six months after I opened, I knew I was going to open the second one. Everyone thought I was crazy—after all, there weren't any espresso bars in Wilmington. How, they said, was I ever going to make money?" But, she did.

By 2000, Alisa had 15 stores, 10 in Delaware and five in Pennsylvania. That's when things started to fall apart. Her marriage ended, some of the locations she'd chosen weren't panning out, and she felt she wasn't doing a good job running the business.

"I was tired of fighting the battle and working so hard to make it all work," Alisa says. "I thought maybe someone else would do better. I brought in a man who was an accountant and an attorney. In two years, he nearly crashed the business. We were close to bankruptcy. He overstaffed everything, didn't give people cost guidelines for labor, and I ended up $2 million in debt. It was bad, and it took me years to pay off the debt. Thankfully, the banks worked with me."

Alisa believes that it's important to talk about these difficult times in her business so that people who want to follow in her footsteps understand that the path to success is never easy—everyone makes mistakes and struggles. What keeps one going is the ability to keep learning and not to lose sight of one's vision.

"I shed the stores that were not making money," Alisa says, "and got rid of the Pennsylvania stories. I went back to my Delaware roots."

After her divorce, Alisa met Chris, a former Philadelphia Inquirer sports writer and attorney who is now a mental health counselor. They have been married for 13 years. In 2003, they adopted their daughter, Kina.

"I never thought I was going to be a mother," says Alisa. "I was just so focused on career and travel. In retrospect, I would have loved to have had more children. I love being a mother. It's the best thing in the world. So, in taking back the management of my business, it was essential for me to give 100 percent priority to my daughter."

Alisa's management style is to hire good people, give them the direction they need, and then get out of their way. "I like working with smart people," says Alisa, who has 120 employees, most of them part---time. She's getting ready to renovate some of her stories, and pour more attention into her new business venture, Brandywine Coffee Roasters, which is a wholesale coffee business. "I've finally found a business that really turns me on, and I wish that for everybody."

Alisa's Final Thoughts

"I have made every mistake possible, and here's what I know:

"Whatever you want to do, do it well. Be good at it. Be an expert. Be obsessed with it. Plan the business, and have a plan for yourself. Know what you want to do in the next three, five and 10 years. Your plan doesn't have to be set in stone. It will change as you go along, but having a roadmap is important

"Treat your mind and body well. Be healthy, because you need energy and creativity. Take good care of yourself. And finally, understand that the most important thing in life is friends and family. Don't let them slip away."

Janice Nevin, M. D., MPH

150

Janice Nevin, M.D., MPH

"It's great if you can get to the table, but it's not enough. You have to figure out how to get your authentic voice into the conversation. You have to work on that. Own it. "

Biography

A visionary and collaborative health care leader, Janice E. Nevin is president and chief executive officer of Christiana Care Health System. She leads with a purpose that is simple yet profound—"We take care of people."

Janice is recognized nationally for innovation in patient- and family-centered care, with patients and their families as partners with health professionals.

Since joining the faculty at Christiana Care in 2002, Janice has advanced the health system's commitment to helping Delawareans achieve optimal health in ways they value and can afford. Through her leadership roles, including chair of family and community medicine, chief patient safety officer and chief medical officer, she led a transformative and strategic shift at Christiana Care, improving quality, safety and patient experience to national acclaim.

Born in England and raised in Delaware, Janice graduated from St. Andrew's School in Wilmington. In 1981, she graduated from Harvard University and earned her medical degree with honors from Sidney Kimmel Medical College at Thomas Jefferson University in 1987. She completed her family medicine residency at Thomas Jefferson University Hospital in 1990 and received her master's degree in public health in community health services from the University of Pittsburgh's Graduate School of Public Health in 1992. She also completed a two-year faculty development fellowship in family medicine at St. Margaret Hospital in Pittsburgh, a program in executive education at Harvard Business School in 2010, and a fellowship in physician executive leadership at the Health Management Academy in 2009.

Janice lives in Wilmington, where she raised two daughters with her husband, Dr. Charles Pohl.

Janice's Story

When you meet Dr. Janice Nevin, enjoying her warmth, ready smile and terrific sense of humor, it's easy to forget her status—or the fact that she runs the largest health care system in Delaware; that she went to Harvard; or that she has won multiple awards for vision and leadership. Instead, you ease into a pleasant conversation.

She has accomplished so much in her life, rising to the top of a field traditionally dominated by men, the formidable competition and rigid, risk-averse bureaucracies. But she shines, innovates and makes wonderful things happen, like establishing Christiana Care as one of the major teaching hospitals in America, or being named one of the top "Physician Leaders to Know" by Becker's Hospital Review.

Yet there she was, sitting right beside me, ordering a salad and talking about her family.

She was born the oldest of three sisters in Cannock, Staffordshire, England. Her parents, both born and raised near Newcastle, England, were from working class backgrounds.

"My father's family has a long history of working in the coal mines." Janice says. "His father drove a delivery truck. They were very much working class."

Her father, Ronald Nevin, left school at 14. In the British school system, opportunities to advance were very limited.

"He had a rich life, but a hard start," says Janice. As a young man, he experienced a subarachnoid hemorrhage (bleeding into the brain). It was unusual for someone to survive such a catastrophic event, but he did. "After leaving school he worked as a rent collector and a taxi driver among other things. In time, he was accepted to seminary and graduated as a Methodist minister."

Ronald met Janice's mother, Sadie, at church. They both sang in the choir. He was 16, and she was 15. "My mother said that she knew the first time she met him that they would get married," says Janice.

Sadie left school when she was 16. "She, too, was very bright and capable, and had been accepted into the secondary school," says Janice, "but her parents didn't want her to have to ride the bus across town, so she went to secretarial school."

Ronald eventually made the decision to join the Anglican Church, which required additional training. The Nevin family moved to Lincoln so that Ronald could attend the seminary at Lincoln Cathedral.

"My sister, Claire, was born there, and after he finished training we moved to a village near Stockton on Tees, where my father was an assistant priest and then to an even smaller village called Cockfield in County Durham, where we lived for four years."

In 1969, Ronald responded to an advertisement in the Church Times placed by an Episcopal priest in Princess Anne, Md. who was interested in an exchange.

Her father was chosen for the exchange. "We lived in Maryland for three months, during the summer," Janice says. "I learned to swim and had my first slice of pizza. I remember sitting on the porch and watching Neal Armstrong walk on the moon on our TV. It was a wonderful time."

Several months after the family's return to England, Ronald was offered a position at the Episcopal Church in Quantico, Md., near Salisbury. He wanted his children to have a better opportunity for an education in a way that he hadn't and, although it was a challenging decision, he accepted.

"I remember being more excited than anxious about the news, because, like my father, I have always loved adventure," says Janice. "But it was the first time I ever saw my mother cry. I was still a child and didn't yet have the capacity to understand what a huge cultural adjustment she had to make. For instance, newly arrived in America, she was asked to cook muskrat at the church dinner."

In England, children start school at four. Because Janice had come from a different educational system, the school officials in Maryland weren't sure where to place her, so they put her in the fourth grade with the other 10-year-olds. She only lasted a day.

"They moved me up to the fifth grade," says Janice. "I was there for a month, and then they moved me to the sixth grade. I graduated from high school when I was 16."

Ronald knew from the beginning that his stay at the Maryland parish would be short-lived. After three years, he took a position at the Church of the Ascension in Claymont, De As the family was preparing to move to Delaware, Ronald learned that St. Andrew's School in Middletown had made the decision to accept girls.

"I loved St. Andrew's," she says. "I was in the first group of girls to attend the school after it became co-ed. There were 26 girls and 180 boys. It was an enormous opportunity to grow and learn. Those years continue to have a lasting impact on me."

Janice describes herself as having been a serious and studious child who learned to read at a very early age. She read everything she could get her hands on—even cereal boxes.

"My sisters used to call me 'bossy boots,' I think because I was bold and confident," she says. "I like to think that it means I showed early signs of executive leadership skills!"

Janice's parents instilled in their three daughters that there was nothing they couldn't do because of their gender. "I grew up believing that anything was possible," says Janice.

Janice says that she'd always wanted to be a doctor, but imagined herself as a country doctor in a rural setting. "When I went to college it was with the intention of taking pre-med courses and applying to medical school," she says. "The funny thing is, I didn't like the pre-med courses. I didn't understand what physics had to do with being a doctor, so instead, I majored in something called 'history and science' at Harvard. It was a major that allowed me to focus on history, particularly the history of health and medicine, while still doing my pre-med requirements."

Her coursework led her to develop an interest in public health and the impact of social determinants on health. Although she had questioned pursuing a career in medicine she recognized that becoming a physician would provide the greatest opportunity to impact health. Her pre-med advisor had concerns.

"After looking at my transcripts (I had a B average)," says Janice, "she told me in no uncertain terms that I should find a different career because I'd never get into medical school."

Despite the advisor's harsh appraisal, Janice decided to pursue her chosen profession. During her Harvard years, Janice rowed on the varsity lightweight crew and was captain in her junior year. She left the team in her senior year.

After graduating from Harvard, Janice spent a year in England on a fellowship from the Wilmington Rotary Club and studied social and economic policy at Durham University.

She didn't get into medical school the first time she applied. "I was wait-listed at Jefferson," she says, and then I got a call from the American School of Switzerland in England. It's a boarding school with an international student body—some of them children of U.S. citizens working in the oil industry in Saudi Arabia. I applied for a teaching job, and because I had a U.K. birth certificate, they asked me to come and teach, and I said yes."

Janice taught algebra and geometry, coached field hockey and crew, and did dorm duty. She loved the school's easy access to London and the rest of Europe. It was a tremendous experience and it taught her a valuable lesson.

"Sometimes things don't work out as you planned—they work out even better," she says. "Every time you experience challenge, there's an opportunity. It depends on what you do with the situation."

Janice graduated magna cum laude from medical school. She was president of the honor society and received several awards for her clinical performance at commencement.

She met her husband, Charles Pohl, now a pediatrician, during student orientation at Jefferson. Their first date was on April 1 the following spring. The rest is history.

"When you graduate from medical school, you apply for your residency. There is something called a 'couple's match.' If you and your partner or husband want to do residencies in the same geographic area, it's possible to stay together. But Charlie wanted to train at Pittsburgh Children's Hospital and I wanted to stay at Jefferson. So for the next three years, we had a long-distance relationship. In the final year of our residencies, he asked me to marry him."

Upon finishing her family medicine residency, Janice joined Charlie in Pittsburgh for a two-year faculty development fellowship that included earning a master's degree in public health from the University of Pittsburgh. After completing all of their training, Janice was hired as a faculty member at Jefferson and Charlie was hired to open the first Nemours community clinic, so the couple moved to Delaware.

"Initially, I was tasked with bringing community-oriented primary care to the family medicine department. Eventually I became the residency director of the family medicine program at Jefferson. This was an amazing job for me as I had the great privilege of working with medical students and residents. I learned so much about leadership and the importance of developing people from this experience. It laid the foundation for the rest of my career."

Today, Charlie is the Associate Provost and Senior Associate Dean for Student Affairs at Thomas Jefferson University and senior associate dean for student affairs at Jefferson's Sidney Kimmel Medical College.

The couple has two daughters. Emma, 23, who graduated from Wilmington Friends School and the University of Richmond and now lives in Charleston, S.C., teaching elementary school. Annie, 21, graduated from St. Andrew's School and is now studying psychology, social entrepreneurship and public health at Wake Forest University in North Carolina, with a year to go.

Janice doesn't believe in the notion of striving for balance in life. "Life is never really balanced," she explains. "I believe that it is possible to lead an integrated life which means understanding priorities and making those constant adjustments which make it all work. Having a wonderful partner in life who shares your sense of humor is a key ingredient!"

Janice describes her leadership style as highly collaborative. She has always gravitated to leadership roles but learned more broadly about leadership when she was asked to run for a board seat for a national organization supporting family medicine residency directors. "Honestly, I didn't think I would get elected but I am so glad that I did – I was exposed to so many great leaders from around the country and had opportunities to get involved in family medicine at a national level. It was transformative and led to several other leadership positions."

One day, she got a call from Dr. Joe Lieberman, then the chair of family medicine at Christiana Care.

"Joe shared that he was retiring and encouraged me to consider applying for the job," she explains. "I told him I was flattered, but I wasn't sure I wanted to make a change. I had always imagined staying at Jefferson for the duration of my career. But I respected Joe and agreed that I would consider the position. After spending at day at Christiana Care I knew that if I was offered the job that I would take it.

"I had never been at an organization that so completely understood its mission—one of service to the community. I've been at Christiana Care for 14 years now, and I remain impressed at the willingness of leaders, caregivers and all staff across the organization to come together to solve problems to further the mission.

"Christiana Care has given me the great privilege of being able to give back to the community which has and continues to be so important to me and my family. It is an honor to work with and serve so many great people here in Delaware."

Janice's Final Thoughts

"There is a huge risk for women when we don't speak up, that of being pushed to the side and not included in important, strategic decision making.

"When I was chief medical officer, I found myself at a meeting at an organization I loved, and one which helped me to get where I am today. There were two women and 15 men, all of us chief medical officers, and a large discussion was taking place.

"The other woman in the room sat across from me. Both of us tried many times to get into the conversation, but every time we would open our mouths, a man would talk over us. When we left the meeting, we looked at each other and asked, 'What just happened?'

"That night, I started to read [Facebook COO] Sheryl Sandberg's book, 'Lean In.' The next morning, I said to my fellow female CMO, 'You have to read this book! We are not going to let this happen to us again. It is our responsibility, not their responsibility, to make sure our voices get in the conversation because both of us have something important to say. We are going to look out for each other. "The next time the group met, we both lived up to the promise we'd made to each other. At the end of the meeting, one of our male colleagues said, 'You know, it's great that we have women here.'"

Robyn Odegaard, Ph.D

Robyn Odegaard, PsyD

"Tell your story with all its hardships and with every scrap of humor you can muster. We're ready to listen."

Biography

Dr. Robyn Odegaard, affectionately known as "Doc Robyn," is a success liaison, TEDx speaker coach, CEO of Champion Performance Development, founder of the Stop The Drama! Campaign, and Organizer of the Happy2Listen movement. She is Delaware's only trained sport psychologist providing coaching, training, and speaking that sets the highest achievers and elite performers apart from their business competition.

The oldest of eight children, Robyn didn't have the opportunity to go to college after graduating from high school. She got her first job in the banking industry, and several years later, was headhunted to start and manage a technology helpdesk. Her last position in the corporate world was working for OnStar, in production support and project implementation for its call center.

Throughout her 14 years in the corporate jungle, people often approached Robyn to share their challenges or get advice. A particularly heart-wrenching encounter with a fellow employee was the motivation she needed to reinvent herself. At 32, Robyn began a focused six-and-a-half- year journey to earn her undergraduate in clinical psychology and master's, and doctorate in business psychology with a concentration in sport and performance.

Robyn has authored two books: "The Ultimate Guide to Handling Every Disagreement Every Time," and "Stop The Drama! The Ultimate Guide to Female Teams." Her philosophy combines the champion-like mindset she developed as a competitive beach volleyball player and her expertise in Emotional Intelligence. She uses her passion for inspiring, teaching and storytelling to help clients and mentees create elite success.

Robyn's Story

Dr. Robyn Odegaard is a woman who takes command of a room from the moment she enters it. She stands tall and exudes confidence, and it was no surprise to me when I learned she had once been a competitive volleyball player and horseback rider. She's got that competitive glint in her eye.

Robyn is the kind of person who admits openly that she's ready and willing to tackle whatever challenges come her way, and she proves this publicly, on a regular basis.

For example, when she and her husband, Russ, decided they wanted to have a large, raised deck on the rear exterior of their home, they didn't call a contractor. They did their research, rented machines, purchased supplies, and then went about building the structure. The project, which she chronicled on Facebook, was no small undertaking. Her house is "all decked out," as she says. Bring on the next challenge.

Robyn's drive to accomplish important goals and stretch beyond her limits fuels her work with athletes and business achievers to re-stoke the fires in their bellies and climb to their next levels of performance. Her grit and determination were instilled at an early age during a rural youth and were further enhanced throughout early adulthood when she realized she had a gift for revving up others' self-motivational engines.

She was born in a small, rural town near Los Angeles, the oldest of eight children. "Mom was a telephone operator," says Robyn. "In those days callers could hear other people's conversations if the operator left the line open. When my father called, she'd keep him on the line to answer other calls, telling him to be quiet. But sometimes he'd break into the conversation, like one time when someone called to tell the operator he was about to pass out, and my father, not being able to help himself, blurted out, 'What happened'?"

Mom stopped working when Robyn was born. "We lived close to my mother's family," says Robyn. "I was one of those kids who would probably be medicated now. When I run into people at my grandmother's church, and they recognize me, they say, 'Goodness, you had so much energy!' One woman complained about how hard it was to babysit me."

Dad had undiagnosed Asperger's Syndrome, a condition characterized by social awkwardness and an all-absorbing interest in specific topics. Robyn recognized it when she started studying psychology. "My father had a very dominant, outgoing personality, says Robyn, "My mother tells a story that she and my dad were at a Christmas party when she was pregnant with me. At the dining table, she waited patiently for dad to pull the chair out for her. When he didn't, she pulled out the chair herself, and then my father sat in it!"

When she was 4, Robyn's father moved the family to a 40-acre dairy farm in central California. They had no money, and the dairy went bankrupt. "We were so poor that we ate road kill," says Robyn. "If one of our chickens wandered onto the road and was hit by a car, my mother picked it up. 'That's five bucks flopping around out there,' she'd say. She was an extremely sensitive soul. It was very hard on her."

Robyn wasn't close to her mother, though. With eight children to raise and the pressures of poverty, Mom became overwhelmed.

"When I was six, she sent my 4-year-old brother and me out to play," she explains. "I decided we should go visit a little girl who lived on a street where my school bus used to go. To me, she lived around the block, so my brother and I set out for her house. We walked about a mile across the fields—I looked it up on Google—which is a long way for little kids to walk alone. Her mom gave us a snack and then sent us back home without offering us a ride. So back we went, and as it turns out, my mother didn't even know we were gone."

Dad, a talented musician, had a master's in music and could play all the woodwinds and brass. In Los Angeles, he'd been a music teacher at a Christian school but became disenchanted with it. When the family moved to central California—Robyn isn't clear on the reasons for the move—he worked as a landscaper, bus driver, and then as a custodian at a school that offered his children a good education.

"None of the kids are musically trained," Robyn says. "When I was in fifth grade, I tried to play the flute and failed miserably. My father told me it was because of the shape of Cupid's bow on my upper lip. It makes it impossible to get a clean stream of air into the flute."

Robyn is very close to her siblings. Three were born after she turned 15, and she feels more like a mother to them than a sister. It's what happens in large families: the oldest children look after the younger ones.

"I watched over the kids inside and outside the house. I was equal to the boys and expected to work just as hard," she says. "As a teenager, I could carry a 50-pound bag of feed up a hill. I can't tell you how many men were shocked when this scrawny, colt-like girl, all knees and elbows, chucked 50-pound bags of feed into the truck with seemingly little effort."

Robyn drove the tractor, changed the oil and fixed it when it broke. She's handy and does what needs to be done. It explains why she and her husband built an outside deck together—a rather big one, by the way.

Inside the home, expectations of her changed from hard labor to housekeeper and a wife who cleaned, cooked and changed diapers. She dreamed of going to college but was told by her father that she was required to live at home until she married, and that affording college was out of the question.

"I knew I was going to have to pay for college myself," she says, "but even so, my father demanded I attend a college that was nearby enough that I could live at home. How was that going to happen when we lived 20 minutes from the nearest, one-stoplight town?"

As she began to grow and mature and become more beautiful, Robyn's father kept his oldest daughter on a tight leash. Because he was a teacher at her high school, he was able to keep tabs. He didn't allow her to date. Robyn once heard him bagging about how she didn't have a curfew. She pointed out she didn't have a curfew because she wasn't allowed to go out.

"He let me enter a beauty contest when I was 17, which I won," she says. "My father says I won because I ran against cows. But I learned a lot from that experience. You can be scared to death, but if you put your head up and your shoulders down, and own it, you'll be OK."

She remembers trying very hard to remain in her father's good graces: beauty queen, A student, star track runner. At times, she felt she failed him miserably, and it turned her into a top competitor, always bringing her best to the situation.

"My father picked my first husband," she says. "I graduated, got married, and moved 3,000 miles away from home within a three-week period. Dad truly felt he was doing good by me, finding someone willing to put a roof over my head, and feed and clothe me."

Unfortunately, it wasn't such a good match, and Robyn was miserable living so far away from her family. Her husband, a pipeline welder, was in debt and had a drug habit; neither of which her father had realized.

"About six months into the marriage I called home," Robyn says. "My little brother, 15 years my junior, told me I'd been away visiting too long and it was time to come home. I just sobbed."

One of the few good things that happened during this union was that her husband insisted she get a job. She found one, working in the back office doing wire transfers for a bank. In the end her husband threw her out for being lazy.

She met her second husband after she'd been recruited to work at OnStar. "He told me I looked good on his arm," says Robyn. "When we'd been married four weeks, I found that his online dating profile was not only active but very much in use. My new husband was a full-blown narcissist; prone to infidelity, pathological lying and other abuse, and it was a painful, roller-coaster relationship that lasted a long, eight-and-a-half years."

Robyn quit her job at OnStar to move to Long Island with her new husband. She couldn't even get an interview for a job because she only had a high school diploma. Her husband said, "We don't need you to work. Why don't you just go to college?" She earned a bachelor's degree in psychology in only two-and-a-half years. Just as she was finishing her husband took a job in London, England. At about the same time, Robyn was accepted into a combined Master's and Doctorate program at Rutgers University in New Jersey.

Her husband moved to London and she moved their household to New Jersey where she purchased a house so she was qualified for in-state tuition. "It worked out well," Robyn explains. "He did his thing in London while I went to school in New Jersey. I only had to see him once every 6 to 8 weeks. It's the only thing that made the marriage last as long as it did."

"I was drawn to psychology for many reasons," says Robyn. "I'd always wondered who I really was and whether I was able to live up to my potential. People had always been drawn to me, wanting to tell me their stories. I loved to listen, and in one particular instance, my having listened helped a co-worker significantly. I realized I could make a difference—help people realize their potential—something I wanted for myself as well."

Because she had competed in horseback riding events in her teens and was a competitive beach volleyball player in her 20s, Robyn developed a fascination for the character and discipline of top athletes, so the organizational psychology program at Rutgers, with a concentration in sport performance, was a perfect fit.

"My internship was divided into two areas: working in the corporate world in an organizational development program for a Tennessee-based airline, and also learning sport psychology by working with the athletes at Rutgers."

Her dissertation was based on creating a team development program for a Division 1 swim team. Her first book "Stop The Drama! The Ultimate Guide to Female Teams" resulted from her dissertation work.

During these years of prolonged marital stress, combined with the urgency to complete her education as quickly as possible, Robyn experienced an epiphany when someone gave her the best advice of her life.

"I was telling somebody a story about some craziness in my life, because I collected craziness," she says. "He said, 'Robyn, you are resilient. Stop making decisions that make you prove it.' Wow! It made me take a hard look at my life and my second marriage. How much of the craziness was my own creation? I created flying monkeys then complained about them. I had to take ownership of that."

Armed with this new insight, Robyn sent husband No. 2 packing. She has made peace with it and the other circumstances of her past that caused pain and confusion.

"I wouldn't change a thing," she says. "Not that I could, but if I were to change my history, it would change me, and then, it would change who and how I help others. I'm very happy now. It's all come to a wonderful place."

Learning how to forgive and reframe the past was the inspiration for Robyn's "Happy2Listen" movement. During a recent holiday season, she took a piece of cardboard, wrote "Happy2Listen" on it, sat in a public space, and waited. Before long, strangers were approaching her to tell their stories.

"For however long they want to share, I give them the space to be whoever they want to be at that moment," she explains. "As a stranger who doesn't know their past, I'm someone who won't judge. It's very special."

Robyn describes her leadership style as collaborative.

"There is a style I like to use called motivational interviewing," she says. "Instead of having a wrestling match in a conversation, have a dance. Ask people questions that allow them to reach a conclusion on their own, rather than telling them what the conclusion should be. It doesn't always mean that they reach the conclusion you want them to have, but the understanding between you and the new ideas that emerge can be awesome."

Robyn has strong opinions, and she expresses them freely without reservation and with complete conviction. One of those opinions is about an expression people use about entrepreneurship: *If being an entrepreneur was easy, everyone would do it.*

"I hate that saying," she says. "Sometimes things are hard, and that's OK. You're allowed to talk about it being hard and be annoyed by it. This saying also disregards the fact that some people have amazing talents that make things easy for them that aren't easy for everyone else. When people assume things that are easy for them are easy for everyone they never use their talents to benefit themselves and others. Life is full of challenges, whether you're an entrepreneur or not and I think it's rude for someone to shrug off someone's concerns by saying "If it were easy everyone would do it." I'm not a 'rah-rah' coach, but I'm really good at saying to someone, 'You can do this!' I love being an entrepreneur, and especially enjoy the challenge of working with a variety of different clients who have different needs and goals."

Robyn has married again. She and her husband, Russ, are fitness buffs who enjoy going to the gym and riding their bicycles together in the summer, sometimes 50 to 100 miles per week. The couple also enjoys ballroom dancing. "We do lots of active things together," she says, "and we also do great work together."

Russ, a self-employed graphic designer, created the look and feel of Robyn's website and designed her second book cover. They met in a gym a few years ago when Robyn lived near Princeton, N.J., and they talk about everything.

"I could brag about him for hours and hours," she says. "The cover of my book, "The Ultimate Guide to Handling Every Disagreement Every Time" was designed during a bike ride," she says. "We talked more about it when we got home, and he drew it in a snap. He's just talented like that. Together, we can solve the world's problems."

Robyn especially likes working with students. She is a part of the Horn Program in Entrepreneurship at the Alfred Lerner College of

Business and Economics at the University of Delaware.

"I've been a judge at some of its entrepreneurial competitions, and have made myself available as someone they can talk to," Robyn says. "I'm also reaching out to the other universities in the area to see if I can adjunct or create a sport psychology program. I would love to work with young people that way.

Robyn's Final Thoughts

I love telling stories. Telling a good story is a family legacy, and my father was a master. He knew all about timing and cadence. I think that's why I'm a coach, trainer and public speaker. It gives me the opportunity to take all the stuff I've learned in the School of Hard Knocks and package it in a story that says, 'Here's some insight you can use.' When I go to a speaking engagement, training room or coaching session, my goal is to help them water their grass so it can grow, then they don't have to worry how green their neighbor's grass is.

My intent is not to be inspirational, per se. It's wonderful, of course, when people tell me I've changed their lives or made a difference. You can't buy that kind of feedback or the feeling you get. I just love telling my story. Storytelling is a passion.

So I say to you: Tell your story with all its hardships and with every scrap of humor you can muster. It sends a message of hope and motivates others to pursue their desires and have courage. People need what you have to offer.

Danielle Rice

Danielle Rice

"Do what you love, and love what you do. Be the best you can be. Find the place that fits who you are."

Biography

Dr. Danielle Rice is the director of the Museum Leadership Graduate program at Drexel University's Westphal College of Media Arts and Design in Philadelphia. She has more than 25 years of experience in designing and implementing innovative, new programs to communicate art to the public.

Danielle, a distinguished advocate for arts education, has extensive experience in all aspects of museum management. She served as executive director of the Delaware Art Museum from 2005 to 2013, working with its diverse range of members and partners to make the museum more visitor-friendly and community-minded.

Before becoming executive director, Danielle worked at the Philadelphia Museum of Art for 19 years, and served as curator of education, senior curator of education and associate director for programs. She oversaw the department of special exhibitions, education, publications, the library and the archives. She has also headed the education departments of the Wadsworth Athenaeum in Hartford, Conn., and the National Gallery in Washington, D.C.

Her approach to museum leadership fits seamlessly with the Westphal College's philosophy of interdisciplinary education and technology. In addition to coordinating exhibitions, she has developed new interpretive strategies for permanent collections throughout her career, engineering large-scale celebrations, scholarly symposia, community outreach projects and technology installations in multiple museum settings. She has authored and produced interactive computer programs, kiosks and websites, random access audio tours and distance education through videoconferencing.

Danielle holds a doctorate in Art History from Yale University and a bachelor's from Wellesley College.

Danielle's Story

I first met Danielle Rice when she was executive director at the Delaware Art Museum. My work as an arts supporter, fundraiser and philanthropist has allowed me to meet some truly spectacular people, including Danielle.

One of my favorite things about her is her effortless charm. She speaks of her convictions with warmth and candor. I envy her students, who, I hope, appreciate that they're learning from a master, someone who has held leadership positions in some of the country's largest and most prestigious museums, including the National Archives in Washington, D.C.

She was born in Bucharest, Romania, to Jewish parents who had survived the Holocaust. Both were pediatricians.

"The year I was born, the Communists were just coming into power, and they were just as anti---Semitic as the Nazis, if not more so," says Danielle. "About a month after I was born, my grandparents, who lived across the street, were coming over to babysit me (because my mother was still in medical school) and they disappeared. They had been taken away to separate Communist reprogramming camps and were gone for two years."

Danielle's mother hired a nanny so she could continue medical school. Her sister, Manuela, was born three years later with serious kidney problems. Danielle's parents wanted to take Manuela to France to visit a specialist, but leaving the country was impossible.

"When I was six, my father was killed in a terrible accident," says Danielle. "He'd been sent to work in the provinces, which was a two-hour bus ride. One night, the public bus jumped the railroad barrier and got stuck."

Danielle's mother was 28 at the time with two young children, and one was quite ill. Her grandparents' lives had been destroyed, because the Communists had taken away their property—at least, what was left of it after the war.

"Because both the bus and the railroad were state---owned, the state offered my mother a large pension," Danielle says. "She negotiated to let them keep the pension if they'd let her go to France with the entire family, enabling her to take her younger daughter to a specialist. State officials agreed, and the family went to France and applied for asylum. We were there for a year, so French is my second language. After that, we came to the U.S."

Danielle's mother was a rebellious teenager growing up in a pre-war era. "She was feisty and sporty," says Danielle. "She was an only child and spoiled to death. Her parents, my grandparents, had been poor but became people of means, because my grandfather owned a bank and a movie theater in the 1930s. This is how my mother was able to afford medical school. After the war, as I said, they lost everything. My mother had such courage! She fought very hard and risked everything to save her family."

Danielle's early school experiences were challenging. "In Romania, one of the challenges during the Communist era was that people spied on one another. In school, kids were encouraged to spy on their parents, and teachers would ask them questions like, 'What do your parents talk about?' I couldn't say anything, because my mother was planning to leave the country."

In France, the family struggled financially, and they ate at a soup kitchen once a week. Danielle was put immediately into school and she had to adjust to a completely different educational system than she was used to.

"They were constantly giving us quizzes, and at the end of the week they posted everyone's class ranking," Danielle recalls. "It was excruciating for me because I didn't yet know the language. I was at the top of the class by the time we left, though."

The family landed in New York, aided by the New York Association of Newly Arrived, which helped them get food coupons. They lived in Greenwich Village for a few months, and then moved to Jackson Heights in Queens.

"I went to fifth, sixth and seventh grades there," says Danielle. "I remember being very eager to fit in and please. In those days, they didn't have any English as a Second Language (ESL) programs, so I learned to adapt fast, which served me well in life. I learned to listen quietly then figure out what needs to be done."

When the family arrived in the United States, Danielle's mother learned that she'd have to redo her internship and residency in pediatrics, a requirement given to all foreign doctors. She decided to switch to psychiatry because it meant not having to take night calls.

"That's when she met my stepfather, the man I call dad, says Danielle. "He had been a pediatrician, too, and he hadn't liked dealing with sick kids and bossy parents. He loves kids—but not sick ones. He decided to switch to child psychiatry. So he and my mother were both older interns in the same program. They got married, and we moved to Westbury, Long Island."

Danielle adored her stepfather, who had become the immediate parent of two children. "He gave us the perfect American childhood," she says. "He loved horseback riding and was a champion sharpshooter, a skill he learned as a member of the Army sharpshooting team. He taught us how to shoot skeet. He bought one of those camper tents, and in summers we traveled all over the country. He was such a cool guy."

Danielle's mother was an early feminist, and the American culture was sharply different than what she'd been used to in a Communist country where women were expected to be in the workforce.

"In America, women were expected to stay at home," Danielle explains, "so the fact that my mom was a doctor was unusual. It inspired her to study feminist psychology, and her work focused on helping women get out of passive roles. I had no doubt growing up that women were equal to men, if not somewhat superior."

She's a self-described shy kid, but also a good listener. "I think it's because my mom talked all the time," she says. "She needed an audience, so I became an audience."

In the eighth grade, Danielle began doing volunteer work for the March of Dimes. She taught physically challenged kids to swim and helped with fundraising. Her neighbor, who had gotten her involved with the charity, said to her: "Dani, I've heard from some people that you're a snob."

"It blew me away!" Danielle says. "I was shocked, but it made me think and search for reasons why people thought of me that way. For one thing, my Dad's father was the superintendent of my school, which made me the superintendent's granddaughter. And when I walked the halls, I clutched my books close to my chest and never looked at anyone. Going forward, I made an effort to look up and say hello to people. I was able to train myself not to look as shy as I felt, and it has served me very well."

Danielle says that she was a "grade grubber," meaning that she was a straight-A student. She also loved art and dreamed of being an artist.

"Doing well in school and being an achiever was a very positive way of getting attention," she says, "and I craved it. My mother had her hands full raising her kids and supporting her parents, who weren't able to get jobs because their English was so poor. She wasn't able to provide the kind of attention I wanted."

She was editor-in-chief at her high school newspaper. "We wrote the paper then printed it," Danielle says. "We had a big press, and did all of the separations, layouts and photography. It was a very cool thing."

Danielle applied to many art schools, but she could tell that her mother wasn't happy about it. "She wanted me to go to Harvard," she says. "Actually, it was Radcliffe back then, and full of incredibly radical people who looked nothing like me. I compromised and went to Wellesley instead, and that pleased her. Sadly, they didn't have an art program, so I fell in love with art history, which is the next best thing."

After graduation, Danielle scored a yearlong internship at The Toledo Museum in Ohio, which wasn't far from Detroit, where she was born.

"I worked in the museum education department," she says. "We were charged with teaching little kids in the galleries about art, and we ran a weekend program. It was very important to me, because when you study art history, you learn how to organize your thinking about who the artists are and how to recognize their styles. When you're standing in front of a real work of art with a group of bright fifth graders, you have to connect them to what they're seeing. I loved that, and still love it."

After her year in Toledo, Danielle went back to graduate school at Wellesley for art history, working as a receptionist at the gallery and teaching art to kids on the weekends. She was a lifeguard during the summer.

About four years out of graduate school, Danielle went to work at the Wadsworth Athenaeum Museum of Art in Hartford, Conn., which is the oldest continuously operating public art museum in the United States.

"One day, out of the blue, I got a call from the National Gallery of Art in Washington, D.C., inviting me to head its education department," says Danielle. "I was amazed! I'd only been out of grad school four years. It was an interesting moment in my career. I mean, how could I turn down the National Gallery?"

The National Gallery post meant she'd go from running a department of five to one of 50. But her gut told her she wouldn't like it there.

"It was a conflict," she says, "because the thing I like most about museum work is talking to and teaching kids. I didn't like the bureaucracy and administrative parts of it much, and I knew there was going to be a lot of that."

But she couldn't say no, and her mother was delighted to be able to tell all her friends where her 32-year-old daughter was working.

"I was replacing a woman who had been there for 37 years," says Danielle. "The place had doubled in size during her tenure, and it required me to do some housecleaning, and I did it, but because the National Gallery is a government organization, I got slammed with paperwork and a bureaucracy like you wouldn't believe. Job descriptions were 45 pages long! When the job at the Philadelphia Museum of Art became available, I jumped ship. I was there for 20 years before going to Delaware."

Danielle likes challenges, so when the opportunity to direct the Museum Leadership graduate degree program at Drexel University presented itself, she took it.

"I had never worked anywhere but in a big museum, so it was exciting to try life as an academic," she says. "I love working with the students."

I asked her whether she'd ever experienced gender discrimination during her career.

"I want to say no, but I think the answer is really yes," she says. "It's hard to pinpoint because I've been lucky enough to work in a field overrun with women. However, it's men who are running the large museums. The discrimination is subtle, but it's there. Luckily, I never had to deal with anything directly, and I was good at what I did."

Danielle met her husband, Jeff Berger, 25 years ago through a personal ad. Jeff teaches philosophy at the Community College of

Philadelphia. The couple has three children—two are Jeff's by a previous marriage, Nora and Alex. Together, they have a daughter named Marcel.

"I love being a parent," she says. "It's what I always wanted. The hardest part was realizing that I'd wanted to be a parent longer than I'd been a child. Then, all of a sudden, they grow up and leave. What?"

Danielle says she's always been comfortable with the work/life balance.

"I've taken good care of my body," she says. "My husband and I get a lot of exercise. I'm on the stationary bike every day, and when the weather is nice, we ride our bikes. But when our kids were small, they were our priority."

She says her leadership style is "consensual." "I like getting different points of view from everybody. I'm not a micromanager, but then again, a micromanager would never tell you he or she is a micromanager. If I did have control issues, I'd attribute them to my mother."

Danielle is enjoying the process of building the museum leadership program. "It's new, but I didn't create it," she says. "I only teach part-time, because my real job is to build the program, bring students in and mentor them. I also create relationships with the museums in the area so students will have a better chance of getting jobs."

Danielle was recently elected chairperson of the board of directors at the Eastern State Penitentiary, a Gothic Revival historic site built in 1829.

"It was born of the idea that prisons needed to be reformed," says Danielle. "Up until that time, prisoners were all thrown together—men, women, thieves, murders and people in bankruptcy. Prisons were just awful places that were just giant holding cells where people waited until punishment could be meted out. Eastern State Penitentiary was created by a group of Quakers who wanted prisons to be more humane. That's why it's called a penitentiary. They wanted prisoners to have time to reflect on what they'd done."

The penitentiary closed in the 1970s, was abandoned by the City of Philadelphia, and subsequently fell into ruin. Preservationists have commenced its restoration.

"It has an extremely successful funding model," Danielle says. "Every year, they create a giant, haunted house called 'Terror Behind the Walls.' It's done very professionally, and it raises 65 percent of its fundraising goal."

Danielle doesn't have many hobbies. "I've been lucky enough to have a job that's fun every day," she says. "I've felt like that with all of my jobs. I can't imagine a life without a job you love."

Danielle's Final Thoughts

"It may sound trite, but do what you love, and love what you do. Be the best you can be. Find the place that fits who you are.

"If I have any regrets, it was that I accepted a position at the National Gallery, even though my gut told me not to. I didn't want to be a cog in a vast bureaucracy. My passion was in the subject matter, not in the paperwork.

"Here's an example: I love having informal conversations about an object on display, and the conversation can last for 30 minutes or more. I wanted to have folding chairs so people could comfortably sit while talking. It took me three months to clear it through security, purchasing and other departments until I could get some simple folding chairs!

"I have a quick-and-dirty, see-what-happens, let's-give-it-a try kind of style, so I didn't fit in there. So I learned to listen to my instincts."

Polly Sierer

Polly Sierer

"I advise kids to choose activities that are out of their comfort zones so they can stretch themselves and build new skills."

Biography

Since November of 2013, Polly Sierer has been serving as Mayor of Newark, Delaware, a university city located 12 miles southwest of Wilmington. Polly is an innate leader and tireless public servant. When she ran for Mayor, Polly followed in the footsteps of her grandfather, a two-term Mayor in Vermillion, South Dakota.

Born in Madison, Wisconsin and raised in Iowa City, Iowa, Polly received her bachelor of science degree in Recreation Education in 1980 from the University of Iowa. She has lived in Newark for more than 20 years.

Polly is passionate about Newark's future, and as such, has been an engaged community leader in the city for decades. She has served on the City of Newark's Community Development/Revenue Sharing Advisory Committee and as a board member of the Newark Day Nursery and Children's Center. Polly is currently the President of the Newark Senior Center Board of Directors and the Newark Area Welfare Committee, as well as a founding member of the Greater Newark Area Interagency Council. She is an avid tennis player and has recently joined the board of directors of the United States Tennis Association---Delaware District. Polly is also an active member of the Newark Morning Rotary Club (Membership Chair), Newark Empowerment Center, Code Purple, and First Presbyterian Church-- Newark. At the state level, Polly has been participating in the Delaware Initiative to End Veteran Homelessness and the Delaware League of Local Government Committee.

Prior to serving her community as a volunteer, Polly worked for two decades in marketing and management for regional property management and maintenance firms, where she handled several large accounts in Delaware and Pennsylvania. She cares about our natural environment and sustainability, and spent eight years as a volunteer and employee at Longwood Gardens.

Polly's Story

Delaware is a small state, geographically speaking, and as is typical of smaller communities, one is likely to run into the same people again and again. The "six degrees of separation" phenomenon doesn't exist here—*two* degrees of separation is more like it. And since I've lived here many, many years, I seem to have at least a nodding acquaintance with almost everyone I meet. It's pleasant and neighborly.

So it's especially fun when I can walk down Newark's charming Main Street and encounter Mayor Polly Sierer, or any city council member or state dignitary who frequents its shops and restaurants.

I've always thought that Polly's job, and, in fact, the job of any close---knit community Mayor must be a tough one. On any given day, Polly is faced with making numerous decisions while considering contrasting opinions. Some constituents benefit by the council's decisions, others don't. And Newark has had its share of contentious situations during her brief time in office.

Polly takes it all in stride. She understood what she was getting into when she ran for office. For her, the role of Mayor allows her to throw her heart and soul into community service, something she was encouraged to do throughout her life.

She was born in Madison, Wisconsin, while her father, Professor Samuel Patterson, was earning his Ph.D. in political science. The family moved to Stillwater, Oklahoma where he taught at Oklahoma State University. A year later, Professor Patterson accepted a position at the University of Iowa, in Iowa City and then moved the family to the Hawkeye State where he was a professor of political science for over 25-years. Professor Patterson later completed his career at the Ohio State University in Columbus. Polly describes her father as a well-known and highly respected educator and author in the field of political science.

Her mother, Suzanne, graduated from Penn State University with a degree in dietary nutrition. She managed the food service departments at both the University of Iowa Hospital and Clinics and at a large hospital in Columbus, Ohio. "Even though she was a very busy and influential woman outside of the home," Polly says, "she was deeply involved in our lives as children. She was involved in the

League of Women Voters and the PTA, as wells as other community organizations. She was a golfer and participated in women's leagues. In addition, my mother was actively involved pursuing the application of Title IX at the state level to ensure that women athletes in Iowa had the rights to equal opportunity in sports in educational institutions that receive federal funds. She encouraged me to pursue anything I believed in, regardless of whether it was popular or something that was considered off-limits to women."

Polly, who has two younger brothers, says she was a tomboy. "I had a paper route and played basketball and tennis. I was a starter, and my mother was at every game, and was always the parent who was willing to help the coach or the team members. I was also very involved at the local recreation center."

As professor of political science, Polly's father Samuel, worked with graduate students, authored books and traveled extensively. "He was very much interested in furthering the education of students at the university and around the world," says Polly. "His expertise was in the legislative process of the United States, so he spent time in Washington, D.C., as well as other countries, making sure that others were afforded fair democratic elections. He was the recipient of the American Political Science Associations prestigious Frank J. Goodnow Award for service to the profession."

Today, at 85, Professor Patterson still has his heart in the game and is concerned with the American electoral process. "I admire him," says Polly, "and subconsciously, many of the choices I've made in life have been influenced by both my mother and father's passion for our sense of community in our cities, states and country.

Polly grew up participating in programs at the local parks and recreation department and loved being outdoors. She remembers annual family camping trips in the summer, riding her bike, hiking and playing tennis. Her family spent their summers visiting and camping in numerous state and national parks. Even at a young age, she dreamed of being a director of a community parks and recreation center. "So naturally, I majored in parks and recreation management at the University of Iowa," Polly says. "My father wasn't thrilled with it—he thought it was a soft topic. Nevertheless, he was supportive of my choice. The skills learned during my upbringing in an active family and my formal education provided me the relationship and leadership skills that have nourished my career in community service.

Her first "real" job was in Texas, working in property management. While her first marriage was brief, Polly, who then became a single mother, emulated her own mother's childrearing skills. "As any single mother can tell you," she says," it's exhausting to be the sole breadwinner while being an involved, loving parent. I spent almost all of my non-working time with my children, getting them involved in activities so they could have a normal, happy childhood. I was always very open and honest with them, always willing to listen, and I'm proud to say they've grown up to be the same way."

The property management company transferred Polly to Wilmington, Delaware, where she eventually remarried to an equally devoted parent who also happened to have two children from a previous marriage. Both had demanding jobs, but they achieved balance by conquering challenges together.

Polly never dreamed of being a Mayor, but after years of her involvement in community service, she realized she could make a positive impact. "Running for Mayor was the hardest thing I'd ever done in my life," says Polly. "I knew very little about running a campaign. I'd worked on a few, but didn't have any idea of what it was like to live in the shoes of a Mayoral candidate. I don't know if anyone can really be prepared for it. You just learn along the way and your skin gets thicker, and yet you can't let yourself become cynical." Polly replaced Vance Funk, III, who'd been in office for just over three terms as Mayor and was a well-established community figure. I wondered if Polly had ever felt intimidated about having had such big shoes to fill, or, since her predecessor was a man, whether she felt she was being treated differently because she was a woman.

"No," she says. "There were other women running, and many women in leadership roles in Newark, so it never occurred to me that I might be filling the shoes of the Honorable Vance Funk. Working with men has never been an issue for me anyway. As far as having felt intimidated, I stepped into the Mayoral role at a time when there was a hotly debated issue that involved the University of Delaware and an organization that wanted to build a data center/power plant on university property. The situation changed the dynamics of the community, and we're healing to this day. It was quite a challenge to get through that period as a newly-elected official who had no previous experience in such matters."

Newark has evolved from a town to a city, with rapid growth that prompted numerous issues, from development to infrastructure, all of which requires change. Human nature resists change, but progress requires it, so the dialogue is often heated.

"I've learned many hard lessons," she says. "First of all, it takes time to accomplish initiatives in a municipality. Knowing all of the facts and becoming educated on all sides of an issue requires concerned citizens to attend city council meetings and ask questions, or engage in dialogue with their city council representatives. Although community input is a vital part of any decision making process, people often jump to conclusions before they understand the full facts and intricacies of a particular issue, especially when it affects quality of life in their neighborhoods. However, I've seen that once people understand all the facts as to why a decision is made, they see the logic and are more willing to participate. My mission is to educate people on how things work, obtain public input and ideas and incorporate the community's voice in city decisions."

Another eye-opening experience for Polly occurred when she reached out to many citizens and business leaders in the community early in her first term as Mayor to arrange one-on-one meetings. Most of them accepted her invitations, but Polly had never imagined that some would decline to work with her on community projects.

"Some people just told me flat out that they wouldn't," she says. "It was part of the skin-thickening process for me. I wanted us to be able to establish relationships and if necessary, agree to disagree. Still, I continue to appoint caring citizens to serve on the city boards and commissions. I believe this was the beginning of the healing process."

Polly also understands the challenge of getting the right services to people who need assistance in the community. She works tirelessly making sure those who need assistance are helped with rent, utility bills, food, shelter, medical needs. "There are significant volunteer efforts going on behind the scenes that people need to hear about," says Polly. "Communication really is the key."

Along the way, Polly read a publication called, "Strategies for Creating a More Collaborative, Effective Council" by the Institute for Local Government. She had presided in the past over meetings for other organizations, but found that chairing city council meetings was different and presented unique challenges. Everything must be discussed during a meeting, in public view. Requirements must be followed, by law, for meeting notification and agenda and minutes posting. Another big adjustment was getting used to generally speaking last.

"We move systematically through the agenda, with council member and public discussion," she says. "Often times, everything I might have said has already been covered and I don't want to bog everything down and repeat it. It takes some getting used to."

She believes her role as Mayor requires a 24/7 commitment, but she wouldn't have it any other way. It's a joy for her, and she feels lucky that the shifts in her home life have made it easier to devote herself to the community full-time. "The kids are grown and living lives of their own," Polly explains. "And my husband's job requires him to do significant travelling. At this point in time our schedules allow me to devote significant time as Mayor of our great city

So, what's so time consuming? I asked. The Mayor presides at city council meetings and attends special events, right? Wrong! "I have a lot of homework," says Polly. "Elected officials should always be researching and reading materials, as well as reaching out to people. City council members are primarily responsible for their districts, but the Mayor is responsible for the entire city. There are many considerations for every decision, and, of course, I can't rely solely on my opinion. I decide based on input from our residents and what's best for the community. It's not easy. I have to separate myself."

Polly says being a mayor is all about leadership, relationship development and doing the right thing. She begins by establishing goals then gathering the right people to accomplish them. She attributes her success to her ability to develop relationships with people from every sector: citizens, business owners, youth, college students, senior citizens, faith communities, low-income families, the homeless and those battling substance abuse, and others. She also continues to develop strong relationships with the University of Delaware and our state and federal legislators.

"When developing relationships with people," she says, "I encourage them to be a part of the process, working on projects or helping with solutions. What I've found is that there are so many people just waiting to be asked to help. They may not be leaders or people who go out and volunteer, but once we've had a chance to communicate and listen to one another, they're willing to engage. That's the grassroots part of being a Mayor in a city like Newark. It's my favorite part of the job and very worthwhile."

Newark is a university city, and its vast diversity of ages, origins and community interests pose special challenges. But Polly feels comfortable in such an environment. "I grew up in a university city," she says, "and it was three times the size of Newark. It had a nice Main Street area, like Newark does. I think that's why I'm so attracted to Newark, because it's very familiar. In a college city, where opportunities abound, people are more willing to try new things and be more creative.

"I know I can make a difference in my community and in people's lives," she says. "I get to work with all facets of the community and that's why I love it. "

But don't try to tangle with her on the tennis court. In fact, prepare to be defeated!

Polly's Final Thoughts

"I'm so proud to say that we have a lot of women in leadership in Newark. I always tell school kids, particularly girls, that if they are interested in being leaders, they should get involved in the community now, as that's what I did in my younger years. It's helpful getting to know many people. I advise kids to choose activities that are out of their comfort zones so they can stretch themselves and build new skills. I tell them my own story, how I approached situations that would require me to speak to groups, because I knew that wasn't my thing. I was happier shooting hoops or playing tennis, and those things didn't require a lot of public speaking. You can do whatever you want with your life, but you have to work at it.

Beverly Stewart

Beverly Stewart

"There are tough times ahead, but your passion will get you through. I've had my rants and tears just like any other business owner, but when you have the passion and the drive, you will succeed."

Biography

Beverly Stewart, M.Ed., is the President and Director of Back to Basics Learning Dynamics, Inc., in Wilmington, Del. She founded Back to Basics in 1985 and was its sole employee. Now, her company employs nearly 200 professionals, offers 60-plus tutoring subjects for children and adults, provides translating and interpreting in 16 foreign languages and sign language, and has served the varied educational needs of more than 16,500 students in the tri-state area. Back to Basics also runs Delaware's only Department of Education-approved one-on-one private school, providing a full curriculum of math, English/language arts, social studies and science, plus traditional and unique electives in an unprecedented teaching environment for students in kindergarten through 12th grades. Back to Basics Learning Dynamics, Inc. has earned a reputation as the area's top choice for all educational services.

Stewart's insights have been featured in national publications such as Entrepreneur Magazine, The New York Times and Consumers Digest. Also, her story has been highlighted in national books including "The Educational Entrepreneur: Making a Difference," and, "What No One Ever Tells You About Financing Your Own Business." Stewart has been a regular contributor on "Your Morning" on CN8, focusing her segments on a variety of educational and parenting topics.

In 1995, Stewart announced the launch of a second business venture: Beverly Stewart Consulting, LLC. She offers business consulting to potential and current entrepreneurs and business owners nationwide, focusing on business start-ups and expansions.

Beverly's Story

Overachiever. Perfectionist. Loner. Studious. Shy. Goody-two-shoes. Beverly Stewart grew up calling herself all of these things.

One of the best parts of writing a book about extremely successful, high-achieving women is having the rare gift of peeking behind the curtain. It's like being allowed a glimpse inside a house you've driven by a hundred times—that colonial cottage on the hill with the charming candles in every window and white smoke rising skyward from the gentle tendrils of its chimney. It's warm and welcoming, yet mysterious.

Beverly's achievements in entrepreneurialism and education followed one after the other since she was in her late 20s, when she sat at her kitchen table and started her tutoring company, Back to Basics. It demonstrates what happens in a person's life when she knows her purpose.

The youngest of three children, Beverly was born in Wilmington, Del., and grew up in a subdivision known as North Graylyn Crest. Her father, William Stewart Sr., worked as a supervisor for more than 25 years at Gates Engineering, a Wilmington-based factory. Her mother, Beatrice, returned to work as a school secretary after Beverly entered the first grade.

"My mother was lovely, sweet, kind, and she was always there for us," says Beverly. "I got my open heart from my mom and my tough, business acumen from my dad. Both of my parents had strong morals and values, although my father was a little on the tough side."

Beverly chooses not to dwell on any of the childhood experiences that were less than positive; specifically, those moments when her father's perfectionism affected the family dynamic and his children's psychological well-being. A proud war veteran with post-traumatic stress disorder, he struggled for many decades to work through his issues. Beverly prefers to take a stoic view and emphasize the positive.

"On the surface, we lived a very traditional life, according to what was going on in the 1950s and 60s," she explains. "Mom stayed home, cooked and cleaned, and dad went to work, collected a paycheck and mowed the lawn on weekends. Life with my father was difficult, emotionally speaking, but it's a double-edged sword. Because of my dad, I developed a love of learning and education. Because of him, I have strong morals and values, and also a tremendous work ethic. Yes, he had issues, and we lived through tough situations, but he also instilled in me many wonderful things, and I am successful because of those traits."

Beverly was shy and reserved as a child, a "good little girl," she says. "I loved arts and crafts, puzzles, books, and anything that challenged my mind. But I was a solitary person, with only one or two close friends at a time, and I wasn't at all comfortable speaking in front of large groups of people. That came much later."

She knew she was going to be a teacher when she was five. "Playing school was my favorite game," she says. "I would gather the kids, who were reluctant, around my chalkboard, and they'd sit in a semi-circle around me. I know it's my calling—I've never doubted it."

There were teachers and mentors along the way who supported her on her path, like guardian angels. "My first- and fifth-grade teachers were especially supportive," says Beverly. "I remember feeling insecure and not very special, and they helped turn my search for perfection into a quest for excellence."

Except for a brief period of rebellion in her late teens (including a stint with a motorcycle-riding older boyfriend), Beverly was a young woman who didn't like to make waves. Yet, a quiet strength grew within her like a sturdy vine, and she began to grasp that she was becoming a strong woman.

"I was in Future Teachers of America in high school, which is about as predictable as it gets," she says, "but what's interesting is that I didn't follow the typical path for someone who loved education and wanted to be a teacher."

Beverly surprised everyone, especially her parents, when she took a year off after high school graduation to decompress and explore other life options.

"Everyone had expected me to go right to college. After all, I had been the star student in the family, a 'distinguished scholar' at high school graduation," says Beverly. "But I needed a break! I worked full time in my senior year in a stationery and gift card store at the Concord Mall, called Matthew's. I had almost all of my credits done by the end of 11th grade and only needed to take two classes in 12th

189

grade. So, when my classes were done at 11:30 a.m., I went to work from noon to 6 p.m."

Her parents gave their blessing when their uber-intelligent daughter said she wanted to take time off between high school and college. "They knew me well enough to know that if I said I'd go back to school, that I would do it," Beverly explains. "And that following September, I was true to my word. My parents paid my whole tuition. They'd saved up their entire working lives and took out loans so that all of their children could go to college, something they'd always wanted for themselves but couldn't afford."

As soon as she graduated from the University of Delaware with a bachelor's degree in elementary education (and subsequently a master's degree in special education), Beverly accepted a teaching position at Sanford School, a private, college preparatory, co-educational Pre-K to 12 day school in Hockessin, Del. She taught the younger students and lived in a cottage on the campus for three of the six years she was there. At 28, she started her tutoring business.

"A colleague at Sanford referred a friend to me who had a son in the first grade who couldn't read well," says Beverly. "There weren't many tutoring companies in the area in the early '80s, so I said, 'Sure!' The little boy came to my little cottage, and I'd tutor him while his mother and sister sat in the other room."

The rest is history. The little boy did so well under Beverly's tutelage that the boy's mother asked her to tutor his sister in a variety of subjects.

"This request watered the seed that had already been planted in my mind," says Beverly. "I was in my fifth year of teaching and wasn't happy in the classroom setting. I knew there was something else out there for me, and I wanted to own my own business. I busily researched other options. I'm very interested in nutrition, but doors wouldn't open for me. Tutoring those children showed me what was right in front of me the whole time—teaching, which I loved, and working one-on-one with students, which was a perfect fit for my personality. So during my sixth and final year of full-time teaching, I also worked four part-time jobs and saved money."

When she made the plunge, Beverly moved into a duplex apartment and pounded the pavements to find customers. She knocked on every door she could think of: doctors' offices, child psychologists, schools. Two principals offered her teaching jobs for which she had no interest, so she countered with an offer to send their students who needed extra help.

"I said, 'If you believe in me that much, then send me students," she says. "I was so busy after four months that I had to hire my first tutor. Back then, there was hardly any competition. Nowadays, it's quite difficult to get the attention of a principal."

Her first years in business weren't easy, but hard times weren't a deterrent. Beverly was determined to make ends meet while she built her business

"I knew I had to make X amount of dollars if I wanted to eat, pay rent and put some money aside," she explains. "More often than not, dinner was a can of green beans. I never ate out, and I did whatever it took to support myself. My priority was growing my business, providing excellence, and working 16-hour days if that's what it took."

Beverly tutored students at her kitchen table, while her first hired tutor worked with students in the dining room. Parents waited in the living room.

"We used every room but the bathroom and my bedroom," she recalls. "After a year, we got so busy that I had to rent a three-bedroom townhouse down the road, where I lived and also had my business. After three years, we filled all of those rooms (two bedrooms were for tutoring), and in the fourth year, we grew so much I had to buy a building."

That building had three stories, and she was there for more than 11 years. "When I bought it I became a landlady," she says. "There were tenants upstairs, and a storefront at its ground floor. I was only 32. I didn't know what I was doing, but I was willing to learn. As my business grew and my tenants' leases ended over the years, I had a contractor build out all the spaces for tutoring. And then I had to rent the garage out!"

In her first year, Beverly's business earned $17,000. Today, three decades later, Back to Basics Learning Dynamics, Inc.'s annual revenues exceed $3 million.

"We do so much more than tutoring now," says Beverly. "We have about 200 people working for us. Most are part-time. I have a whole translating and interpreting division that I began to build up six years ago, and it has blown through the roof."

Working with state agencies and large clients such as Christiana Care Health System, the translating and interpreting services division accommodates 16 foreign languages. "About 85 percent of the company is dedicated to a variety of contract work which also includes tutoring, speech therapy, occupational therapy, psychoeducational testing, and homebound services," says Beverly. "It's not just parents and adult learners coming to us, but also districts, individual schools, the government and the state. We're a comprehensive educational services company now."

Beverly says she is always evolving. She's not the same quiet, shy person she was as a child. For example, after 37 years of teaching and running a business, she is comfortable and adept at speaking to large groups or one-on-one with community leaders and other accomplished individuals. Her business approach also evolves frequently to meet the needs of the educational environment.

"My mantra is 'win-win,'" she says. "If my employees are winning and my clients are winning, then all is well. I may not have had a lot of different places of employment during my career, but I've had thousands of bosses. I think of myself as middle management. My success depends on serving both sides. It's a constant balancing act. I'm very open to people around me speaking up, presenting new ideas, creating new processes and expressing how they feel about the company. We don't do exit interviews. We do 'stay' interviews. I'll ask, 'Why do you stay here?' It's no good asking when a person wants to leave. It defeats the whole purpose, and I may have lost a really good person."

Beverly conducts 'stay interviews' every six to 12 months, asking key personnel to fill out two---page questionnaires about what motivates and de---motivates them, what they like about their jobs, what changes they'd like to see, and what would cause them to leave.

"About 95 percent of people say they love it here," says Beverly. "I like to see retirement or a mismatch of philosophies as the number one reason they'd leave the company. When someone says they would leave the company in order to grow, I pay serious attention. Growth is very important to our culture. I also think new blood is important. It keeps all of us from resting on our laurels, and gives us new ways to see the world and what's going on out there. I'm very grateful for the diversity of our team and the opportunity to see the company from employees of all ages, from 25 to 75."

Like most of the women we've interviewed for "Pearls," Beverly strives to find a balance between running a business and living a full, personal life.

"I take more vacations than I used to," she says, "and for me, a vacation isn't taking days off and staying home. My vacations are five days or more off the grid. I remove myself physically from the area, out of the country if possible, and I don't take my cell phone. Whatever happens can be handled by my staff or wait until I get back. If an employee quits, I don't want to know it while I'm away. If the building catches fire, I trust them to call the fire company. It isn't easy staying out of it, though! I'm the type of person who wants to jump right in. I'm working on that."

Beverly says that learning how to get out of her own way has always been a challenge, but it's a remnant of the perfectionism that was instilled in her as a child. She realizes she's capable of slipping into micro management. "I've asked my staff to help me with this and have empowered them to remind me when I might be overstepping. They are extremely talented and capable people, and they know I trust them."

Michael, a man Beverly met three-and-a-half years ago through their mutual interest in fitness, also provides Beverly with balance and a rich, fulfilling personal life. The two tied the knot in Italy in June, 2016.

"Michael was the COO of a billion-dollar company and retired at 52 to later start a non-profit dedicated to teaching yoga to individuals affected by trauma," says Beverly. "He teaches in juvenile detention centers, prisons, V.A. hospitals and drug and rehabilitation centers. I've been practicing yoga of and on for well over a decade now, so we're aligned in many ways—the drive to serve people, to stay fit and to pursue personal growth."

Beverly's Final Thoughts

"I always tell people to follow the passion in their hearts. Do you want to start a business? Go for it! Don't study too much beforehand, though, because you may not get started. And of course, do it for yourself, and not for others. If you do it for others, chances are you won't stick to it for the long haul. There are tough times ahead, but your passion will get you through. I've had my rants and tears just like any other business owner, but when you have the passion and the drive, you will succeed.

"As far as parenting is concerned, I've seen quite a few disturbing changes over the years. There's helicopter parenting, with parents hovering over their children's lives perhaps a bit too much. And then there's the opposite: parents who leave the upbringing of their children to others. There's an absence of discipline and solid values taught, in my opinion. Some children are allowed to run the household and make important decisions, while parents want to be their child's friend, not parent. Too often I hear, "I just can't get him to do his homework." Wow! That wasn't even an option when I was growing up. Many of my inner staff are my age, and they say the same thing. We would have been killed for not doing our homework! "Now, I'm not saying parents should rule with an iron fist (it has a downside), but consistent teaching of morals, good judgment, and responsibility are key to raising successful children.

"When you walk into our headquarters, there are large, carved wooden letters sitting atop a tall cabinet: R-E-S-P-E-C-T. That word says everything about me, and what I believe and value."

About the Author

Fred Dawson is a writer, musician, businessman, speaker, antique car collector and community leader. He has written hundreds of articles for local, national and international publications and has appeared on both radio and national television programs.

In 1961, at the age of 11, Fred Dawson's mother bought him a clarinet and ignited in him a passion for music that has been a major source of joy his entire life. He started playing professionally at age 16 and began recording at age 17.

In his early band days, Fred also played sax. His bands appeared as warm up concert acts for the likes of Poco, Chicago, Dr. Hook, and many others. He made numerous TV appearances and toured from Hollywood to Maine.

Many years later, Fred played four concerts with "Yakety Sax" man Boots Randolph, a major part of the "Nashville Sound" for most of his professional career. The two became very close friends until Randolph's death in 2007. Boots' family presented his famous saxophone to Fred, who displays it prominently in the music room of his Yorklyn, Delaware home.

Fred has attended several Rock 'n' Roll Fantasy Camps and has performed with Micky Dolenz of the The Monkees, Spencer Davis of the Spencer Davis Group, Liberty Devito and Mark Rivera (drummer and saxophonist for Billy Joel) and many others. He met Ringo Starr for two nanoseconds in 2003 before one of his shows.

In his fifties, Fred started Club Phred, a group of accomplished musicians delighted with 60s and 70s Classic Rock. Club Phred has won numerous awards from the Delaware media and since 2004 has helped various charitable organizations raise more than $2.5 million. Check out www.clubphred.com.

Executive vice president of Bassett, Dawson & Foy, Inc., Fred has over 30 years of wealth management experience and has dedicated himself to being a trusted advisor to successful women.

Fred and his wife, Louise, have two children and five grandchildren.